Sour Face

M J Cox

M J Cox

All rights reserved, no part of this publication may be reproduced by any means, electronic, mechanical photocopying, documentary, film or in any other format without prior written permission of the publisher.

Published by
Chipmunkapublishing
PO Box 6872
Brentwood
Essex CM13 1ZT
United Kingdom

http://www.chipmunkapublishing.com

Copyright © M J Cox 2008

Sour Face

Two thirty am. I stumbled in through the front door. I'd been out with Jill, my best mate. I arrived home later than usual. We were having such a good time, just the two of us.

The house was in darkness. Obviously he was not back. I fumbled with the light switch in the hall. Pulling my phone from the back pocket of my jeans, I rang his mobile. There was no reply. The phone went straight to his voice mail.

I left him another message" Hi, it's me. I am now at home. See you later". I was concerned. He'd been out since 2pm, with "the boys", to watch a professional snooker final. "No women were allowed". The plan was then to have a "few beers" in town. It was now two forty five. That meant he'd been drinking for ten hours. I put that thought to the back of my mind as I turned off the light and went up the stairs to bed.

I was woken by the feel of tapping on my left shoulder, softly at first, increasing in speed and force until I opened my eyes. He was standing at the side of the bed. He appeared to be drunk.

"What time is it?" I asked him, half asleep. "Four o'clock." He replied. His speech was slurred." I'm fucked. We've been all round the town and went in to lots of bars. All of the places were crawling with MULF (Mothers you'd like to fuck). I had the usual attention; they were after a younger bloke to give them a good time." He moved to the other side of the bed, taking the change out of his jeans pocket.

"You should have come with me to the final. You would have enjoyed it. We will have to go soon. I will take you to the next tournament".

I turned over onto my side, replying," I thought the snooker was a boy's only event".

He grabbed my shoulders and turned me onto my back, "Sour face bitch, stupid cunt," he shouted. "You have always got to answer me back. You have got to have the last fucking word. You never show me any fucking respect".

He was now kneeling over me; I was still on my back, pinned down by his body.

He grabbed me by the neck, squeezing my windpipe with both of his hands. I tried to slap his hands away; he let go of my neck, took my left hand, and bit me on the forearm,

"Whore, sour face fucking bitch, I am going to bite you again, and that'll teach you to be a cunt to me." He took my arm and bit it again harder. I tried to pull my arm away, but couldn't move due to his body weight.

"Please stop", I was crying now, "I'm sorry I upset you, I didn't mean to disrespect you, I have been drinking, I am really sorry."

He lowered his head, so his face was level with mine. He stared at me; I could see his eyes, big, unblinking, and hard.

"Fucking whore", he spewed the words out, his spit hit my eyes, and I could feel his breath across my mouth.

He moved his head from out of my face. He raised his arm and hit me.

The first blow was across the right side of my head, catching my ear and cheekbone. This was quickly followed by another harder strike to the same side of my face, lower down near the jaw line. Both times I was struck with such force that I

Sour Face

saw flashes of light in front of my eyes. I began to cry, trying to wriggle away from him; He kept me pinned in position by his knees.

"Please stop, you'vet hit me so hard that I have seen stars", I pleaded with him.

"You will see more than that you fucking bitch", he was ranting, in a real temper. The next blow was again to the right side of my face across the eye and cheek. I was sobbing now; I covered my face and head with my hands.

"Move your hands, sour face cunt. I'm not going to hit you again. Just move them stupid bitch."

I did as I was told. The last blow was to the same right-sided area. Again I saw stars. In my eye level I could see the right side of my face; my cheek had already begun to swell. He moved from me, and I curled up in a ball on the bed, crying so hard.

"Please stop", I begged him.

"Get up then stupid sour face, lying there like a cunt ". I got up and began to walk across the bedroom.

"Where you going?" he stood in front of me.

"I'm just going to the mirror" I replied.

He followed me and stood behind me whilst I looked in to the mirror on the wardrobe door. I could see his reflection looking back at me as I examined my face. He stared back at me, his face showing no signs of any emotion.

"Your face looks a mess ", he told me "that's the trouble with you, you just don't show me enough fucking respect. You always have to spoil everything with your sour face comments. Say you're sorry for disrespecting me".

"I'm really sorry, that's the last thing I want to do, and I promise I will never behave like that again," I was crying again. I just wanted the aggression to stop. I would have done anything to make it stop, anything.

"That's OK. I forgive you this time, but you can't go on treating me in this way. You're always putting me down, acting like you're superior to me, and treating me like a cunt. You have got to stop it .Its wrong".

I said I was sorry again and moved past him heading towards the bedroom door.

"Where do you think you're going now?" He stood in front of me blocking my path.

"I just need to go to the bathroom, I feel really sick". I could feel the bile rising up in my throat. "All right then, you can go". He let me pass but followed me into the bathroom standing in the doorway, as I knelt in front of the toilet bowl; vomit now flowing from my throat into my mouth. "You don't realize how hard it is for me. I think I'm losing my sex drive; I'm not getting any younger. You're no help to me at all. You don't reassure me, or make me feel good about myself. All you care about is yourself. You are all ways making sour face comments. You're a selfish sour face bitch".

I got up off my knees, wiping my mouth with toilet paper.

"Look at the state of you. You look awful. There is always something wrong with you; you are always a fucking drama queen. Stop puking. I can't bear it when you're fucking throwing up, it gets on my nerves."

I threw the paper down the toilet pan, pulled the

Sour Face

flush and stood in front of him. He again blocked my path. "Where you going now bitch? Don't think you're leaving this house. Where's your keys and phone?" he demanded."I'm not leaving; I'm going back to bed. My keys and phone are in the bedroom on the dressing table". I replied.

I wanted him to stop. Stop talking, to stop shouting. Stop hitting. I wanted the abuse to stop.

He followed me back into the bedroom. He checked the dressing table to make sure my house keys and mobile phone were where I'd said they would be. He stood there while I got in to bed. He lay on the top of the bed fully clothed. His shoes remained on. He turned to look at me.

"Your face is going to be a mess. You shouldn't have spoken to me like that. You know I've been drinking all day. It's your fault."

"Don't worry about it. It'll be all right. Just go to sleep now. You must be really knackered. I'm sorry for upsetting you." I wanted him to be still, to be calm. Agree with him. Always admit you're wrong, even when you're right. This was the guaranteed way to instill peace into the situation.

He closed his eyes." Say good night then, or aren't you talking to me? Are you sulking like a typical woman?" He asked me in a mocking voice.

"No I'm not sulking, good night".

I lay still, as still as I could be. I watched his face, for any sign of movement. He lay on his back with his eyes closed. After what seemed like a lifetime, his breathing began to change. His chest rose up and down gently. A soft snore came from his mouth, followed by a louder one, then a snort. He was sleeping.

I gently slid out of the bed. I stood up slowly. I remained standing there at the side of the bed for a few seconds, watching him for any signs of movement. . He always slept nearest to the door, so I needed to get across the bedroom to leave. I crept to the doorway, grabbing the clothes I'd taken off earlier, and my house keys and mobile phone from the dressing table. I slowly walked out of the bedroom, closing the door, so it was slightly ajar.

I stood outside the bedroom door listening. My heart was pounding in my chest. I was expecting him to come out at any minute .I couldn't hear any sound of movement. I went down the stairs as quickly as I could. I opened the front door. Grabbing my work handbag from the coat hooks hanging in the hallway, and my shoes from the hall I tossed them outside, onto the drive. I closed the front door gently behind me and pulled my clothes on as fast as I could. Once I was dressed, I picked up my bag, rammed my feet in my shoes and walked as fast as I could out of the drive and on to the street. I then ran down the hill, looking over my shoulder constantly, tears now pouring down my cheeks, I didn't stop running until I reached Darren and Jill's house.

Sour Face

CHAPTER ONE

After drinking several jugs of cocktails, my friends and I ended up in our local club.

We carried on drinking and dancing into the early hours. My best friend Jill's boyfriend, Darren, arrived at the club. They both went to the bar, and my other friends were dancing, leaving me standing alone.

That's when he came over to me.

He was with a gang of men of various ages, known as "the boys". They were dancing in a large group.

"Is my mate bothering you?" he asked me.

I just ignored him. I thought he was being an idiot. As I've said I was standing alone.

He went back to his friends. I moved from where I was standing, nearer to the bar area, where I could attract the attention of Jill and Darren. They were still waiting in the queue to be served.

He came back over to me. "I've been dancing all night. I'm really hot and sweaty I must look a real mess. God look I'm sorry. I'm not very good at this chatting up business." He smiled at me, and I melted.

"I'm not a very good dancer, as you've probably noticed, but would you like to dance with me?" he asked.

"Alright, just make sure you don't stamp on my toes", I teased him.

He held out his hand. I took it and we went on to the dance floor. We danced together for the rest of the night.

When the club closed, we stood outside chatting.

He told me his name, he was in his late twenties, had worked in various parts of Ireland for a number of years, and had returned to live locally about three years earlier. He had worked in various jobs but was currently working in the main branch of the city library, as a library assistant. He was single and had been for the past two years. In return I told him about myself. I was six years older than him, and had been divorced for five years. I was currently working for social services in the day service department. He asked me my plans for the next evening.

"I'm not really doing anything. It's my day off and I usually spend those sleeping", I answered.

"Would you like to go out with me? I'll meet you in town and we could just go for a few drinks".

I said yes never expecting to see him again. I thought it was one of those situations, where you had a fun evening, said goodnight, and went your separate ways. I gave him my home telephone number, written in eyeliner on a till receipt I found at the bottom of my handbag. We kissed goodnight, I got into the cab with my friends and went home.

The following afternoon, the persistent ringing of the telephone woke me up. I got out of bed to answer it. It was him. I couldn't believe it.

"Hello, I didn't think I was going to hear from you", I was very surprised.

"I told you I'd give you a ring that's why I asked for your number. Would you like to come out with me tonight? There's a really nice restaurant in the student part of town. The food is supposed to be very good. You do like seafood I hope?"

Sour Face

"My favourite ", I replied. "Yes, I would like that very much. Where shall I meet you? I'll take the bus into town rather than drive. That means I can have a glass or two of wine, If my stomach let's me after the amount of alcohol I had last night", I joked.

"Yes, I know what you mean. My head's still a bit thick from last night. I didn't plan on driving either. Shall I meet you at the bus station about seven o'clock?" he asked.

"OK. That's a good time for me. I'll see you then".

"I'll look forward to it", he answered as he hung up.

I reached the bus station just before seven o'clock, to find him waiting for me. He smiled broadly as I walked towards him.

"Hello, so good to see you again", he said warmly as we hugged each other. "I was worried that you wouldn't turn up".

"I wouldn't do that to any one ", I replied.

"You look really nice", he told me with a warm smile. "Are you hungry?"

"I'm starving. I haven't eaten all day", I replied returning his smile.

"I love a woman who enjoys her food and still maintains her figure. The table is booked for seven thirty. We'll go straight there", he said taking my hand as we walked to the restaurant.

We talked all night, about anything and everything. He appeared to be charming, articulate, intelligent and attentive. At the end of the evening he walked me to the taxi rank and waited with me until the next taxi pulled in. We arranged to meet the following afternoon at a local park.

We spent the following afternoon walking, talking,

and sitting in the sunshine. He hired a small rowing boat and we went rowing on the boating lake. The whole afternoon was just perfect.

We enjoyed being in each other's company and arranged to meet again the following weekend. I liked him.

That evening he phoned me to check I'd arrived back safely. He rang me every evening until we saw each other again. The courtship that followed was a whirlwind of romance. We enjoyed intimate meals out in cozy restaurants; we made trips to various museums and art galleries. We went out to nightclubs and danced to cheesy disco music until the early hours of the morning. We spent long lazy mornings in bed: reading the newspapers, watching movies or making love.

He would constantly tell me I was beautiful, elegant and very sexy. We talked for hours. He told me he wanted to be in a real relationship where there were no secrets from the other person; consequently he wanted to know everything about me. This included my childhood experiences and past relationships, including the sexual details. I felt so comfortable with him that I told him everything he wanted to know.

He appeared to be so caring, so interested in my life and me. He also appeared to be so sensitive. A quality I hadn't come across in a man before. He even cried at romantic movies, in front of me, which I found so charming.

On the fourth date, at a museum, he told me he had fallen in love with me. He hadn't meant for it to happen, but it had and he couldn't ignore it anymore. He had been really hurt by previous

Sour Face

relationships and wanted to make sure that his next one would be successful. He was drawn to me, as he found me so warm and loving, qualities that no one had displayed towards him before. He believed that I was "the one", the person he would spend the rest of his life with.

Within two months we were living together.

We had been seeing each other for a few weeks. He had a key to my home. I had been called into work when he rang me from my flat.

He was very angry his voice was raised and his tone was sharp.

"I can't believe you've kept a photograph of your ex boyfriend in your drawer!"

I was taken aback. "What photograph in what drawer? I asked.

"In the computer desk drawer", he replied.

"What are you doing looking through the drawers of my furniture?" I was getting annoyed with him.

"I was just looking for a pen. Why, you haven't got anything to hide have you? If you haven't then it shouldn't be a problem to you where I look. We promised each other there would be no secrets from each other or have you forgotten that?" he asked me.

"Of course I haven't forgotten and I certainly don't have anything to hide. Where was this photograph anyway?" I was curious. I was convinced that I had thrown them all away.

"It was at the back of the desk, in between the two drawers", he replied."I'm sorry if I upset you. I do get jealous, and I got very jealous when I saw his picture. I hate the thought of you being with someone else. I really thought that you had hidden that photograph from me because you still cared about him. I'm very sorry for getting angry. I really love you". He sounded so remorseful.

"That's OK, don't worry about it", I reassured him. "I promise you I haven't kept any pictures of him. That one must have fallen down the back of the drawer. Throw the stupid photograph away and I'll see you when I've finished work".

At the time it didn't occur to me that he had been searching through my belongings. Given the location of the photograph he would have not found it unless he had physically taken the drawer out of the desk.

He was waiting for me when I returned back to my flat. He was pleased to see me. He hugged me warmly.

"I'm sorry if I appeared angry before. You mean so much to me I wouldn't upset you for the world. He said as he held me tightly against him.

"Don't worry it's all forgotten ", I reassured him.

"Have you kept any gifts that he gave you?" he asked me as he released me from his arms, and sat down on the sofa.

"He didn't buy me many gifts. We weren't together for very long. There are a few CD's in the rack that he bought for me".

"I want you to throw them away. I can't bear the thought of you keeping anything that he has bought for you. You are my woman now, not his", he was very passionate. His voice was slightly raised.

"Hang on a minute. I'm not a possession. I don't belong to anyone. Why should I throw the CD's

Sour Face

away? I still listen to them. Don't you wear a jumper that your last girlfriend bought for you?" I was beginning to get annoyed with him.

"That's different. It's an expensive designer top that she bought for me from a European fashion show. I like it I'm not going to throw it away just because I have a new girlfriend. CD's are different. Those ones there you can buy for less than ten pounds now. You can replace them easily. The only reason you want to keep them is because he bought them for you and they are of sentimental value."

"That's not true. I have no sentimental attachment to a couple of CD's, I promise you. If you feel that strongly about it I'll throw them away. It's no big deal. I'll replace them when I get paid"

I just wanted to prove to him that it was him I cared about not some ex boyfriend.

"Thank you. That would mean a lot to me if you would do that for me".

He hugged me "Shall I get them for you now. I'll help you take the bag to the dustbin it looks a bit heavy".

He collected the CD's from the rack and handed them to me. He watched as I dropped them into the bin bag, and then tied the bag shut. He held the door open for me as I carried the bin bag outside and placed it in the communal bin area.

The day after he had told me he loved me he had a beautiful flower arrangement delivered to my flat.

When he arrived to take me out for dinner, I hugged him.

"They are absolutely gorgeous. Some of them are

so unusual. Thanks so much. It really is a nice gesture". I was touched by his kindness.

"I asked for the best ones in the shop. I wanted to get you something really nice, because you are so special to me. Of course if you want the best you have to pay for the best".

He took the receipt out of his wallet and showed me how much he had spent. I was very embarrassed. I didn't know what to do. I just did my usual thing, and made a joke out of the entire situation. That was the first and last time he ever brought me flowers.

To the outside world we appeared to be the ideal couple. An attractive well suited couple, articulate, intelligent and friendly.

My friends liked him. They thought he was a "babe", "never thought tall dark and handsome men existed in real life", and "How lucky are you having a man who is as cute as that" were a few of the comments I received. They as I did at the time interpreted good looking as being a nice person.

There have been several experiments and pieces of research carried out on how society reacts to attractive looking people. It has been proved that good-looking individuals get better care within the health service; attractive women are more likely to be helped by strangers if they are in distress, and good-looking people are considered to be better at their jobs than their unattractive counterparts.

I had never been involved with anyone as attractive as him before.

At the beginning, I felt good about myself. I felt

attractive and special so proud that someone as good looking as him would fancy me.

I could see that he had a few emotional issues, (he had a quick temper, was worried about not having enough money and was jealous of my previous boyfriend) but I thought these would be things that I could manage and with my reassurance and support would be easily resolved.

I never thought that he was a domestic abuser. They were rough, uneducated, ugly people, who lived on a council estate and were unemployed.

He didn't fit that description I had created in my head.

There is no typical domestic abuser as there is no typical victim. They come from all classes, races, professions, ages and educational backgrounds.

I really believed that domestic abuse didn't happen to women like me, educated, professional women.

I would never allow myself to be treated in an aggressive way, I could stand up for myself and wasn't afraid to do so. I had no knowledge of the emotional conditioning and control that goes hand in hand with the violence of domestic abuse.

I owe an enormous apology to all of the women I have judged in the past regarding their tolerance of domestic abuse. I just didn't have any understanding of what they were emotionally going through.

Most people remember the firsts in their relationships. The first kiss, the first time you hold hands, the first date, and the first night you spend together. I remember when he hit me for the first time.

We were just about to move into together. We'd been out drinking till late. It was a Saturday morning; we were both hung-over. He was still a bit drunk if I'm honest.

He began to argue with me.

"You looked like an old fucking tart last night. I don't like you going out dressed like a whore", he snarled the words at me.

"No, I didn't."

"That top was far too low, showing all your tits. I saw men looking at you. That's why you wore it. All you want is fucking attention from any man. Sad slapper, old cunt"

"Don't call me that I hate that word," I answered back.

'It's only a word. Look at you making a fuss over a fucking word. Look at you, Miss fucking prim. You really are a stupid bitch". He stood in front of me, staring into my eyes.

"Don't speak to me like that. I'm not stupid. I don't want you calling me names, particularly using that word, the worst name you could call anyone." I stared back at him, holding his gaze.

He lent into my body space, so his face almost touched mine.

"One thing you've got to fucking learn bitch, is that you don't answer me back. You've got no fucking right to scream at me. Who do you think you are? You are just a fucking sour face cunt. Nobody answers me back, particularly a bitch like you. Do as you're told and we'll be just fine, cross me and you'll find out what will happen". He shouted the

Sour Face

words at me. I felt a mixture of beer breath and spittle across my face.

"No, I'm not going to do as I'm told. I'm not a child and I'm not screaming at you". I was angry with him."Who do you think you're talking to mate? I'm not putting with that rubbish, from you or any one".

He leapt forward, grabbing my neck with both of his hands; he squeezed my windpipe, forcefully.

I struggled, trying to knock his hands away from my neck. He squeezed my neck tighter.

"I told you bitch, you don't answer me fucking back. I am telling you not to fucking push me. In fact I'm warning you", he snarled.

I began to cry.

He let go of my neck. He stood back looking at me with disgust. "You are a typical fucking woman. That's right turn on the water works, when you can't get your own way. You're all the same".

He raised his hand and slapped me full across the left side of my face. He then grabbed both of my arms at the top, near the shoulders, and shook me really hard causing my head and neck to rock forwards and backwards.

"You are a sour face bitch. Whore. Couldn't help yourself could you? You just don't know when to shut up".

It was the first time any human being had ever laid a hand on me. I was stunned, upset and shocked by the entire situation. It was surreal.

I was sobbing really hard, sitting on the edge of the bed.

He was very remorseful.

"I'm really, really sorry. I'm still drunk from last night. I don't like being spoken to like that by a woman. You were completely out of order. You provoked me. "

He began to cry. "Please don't leave me. I really love you. I'm feeling so insecure, because we're living apart. I miss you. It'll be better when we live together. I'll feel more settled."

I found myself apologising for my behaviour. Taking the responsibility for what happened. I believed that if I hadn't answered him back, if I hadn't argued with him he wouldn't have hit me. I felt it was my fault. I know now it wasn't.

I was left with severe bruising on my arms. I hid them by wearing tops with longer sleeves. My face had finger mark bruising along the left cheekbone. I covered it up with makeup. I told work colleagues that I'd fallen into a door. I know, that old chestnut, but I really did say it. It had started already, me hiding the physical evidence of his behaviour.

He continued to apologise for the rest of that day. He continuously told me how sorry he was and how much he loved me. He repeatedly told me he would never hit me again because he had never loved any one the way he loved me.

I believed him. I believed him because I wanted to. I wanted someone to love me. So I forgave him.

Researchers have examined the way victims indentify with their abuser. Dutton in 1995 describes a theory called traumatic bonding, which is seen in victims of child abuse, domestic violence and people who have been held hostage. He describes traumatic bonding as "the development of strong emotional ties between two persons, with one person intermittently harassing, beating, abusing or intimidating the other".

Dutton states that there are always the following two features present when traumatic bonding appears:

1. Power imbalance. The abuser has the power in the relationship, and is aware of this. The victim can see the power slipping away from them.

The abuser needs the victim to make them feel powerful. The victims need the powerfulness of the abuser in order to deal with their own feelings of vulnerability. This cycle of thinking can lead to strong emotional ties.

The power does shift in the relationship. After an aggressive episode the abuser will show his regret and shame and will feel powerless if the victim discards them or leaves the relationship. The victim's sense of power improves. The abuser will then try to get the power back either by persuasion or by bullying the victim. This is why victims are sometimes at greater risk of violence when the relationship has just ended.

2. Intermittent nature of the abuse. The victim suffers periods of severe emotional and physical abuse followed by ordinary "normal "periods of time in the relationship. This intermittent nature of the abuse can make the victim feel that they have some control or influence on the abusers behavior and make them believe that he will one day stop being abusive. The victim will enjoy these pleasurable periods of time,

as they will feel relief due to the halt in the cycle of emotional and physical aggression. The mixture of these conditions makes up a strong "behavioural cocktail" In behavioural psychology this is called "intermittent schedule of reinforcement". Any reinforcement of behaviour increases the chances of it happening again.

3.
By taking the aggression out of the relationship and by increasing the pleasurable periods of time in between the abuse the behaviour is reinforced or strengthened, which in the case of the victim is commitment to the relationship. This enhances the emotional tie between the abuser and the victim. Behaviour that is irregularly reinforced is very difficult to change.

Information taken from a training manual for health care professionals makes the point that "victims of domestic violence confuse the effects of traumatic bonding as love".

As soon as we moved in together we stopped doing the things that couples do. We didn't go out for a meal or for a drink on our own. He always had to go out every Friday with his friends; and get very drunk. He would not go out with me on a Saturday evening, even if I hadn't been out on the Friday evening. "Not my fault you haven't got any mates to play with", he would sneer. He didn't like me drinking in the house, not even a glass of wine with a meal. He didn't like me drinking at all, as he'd compare me to his mother when she was drunk. On the rare occasions I did get drunk he

Sour Face

would pick fights with me and because I didn't care, I would really answer him back. That was a big mistake. That would be when he would really hit me. The alcohol numbed the pain.

He would only go to nightclubs with his friends. He refused to go with me. He would then come home, wake me from a deep sleep to tell me how attractive he was, how lots of girls were chatting to him, what a good dancer he now was and how he'd been dancing with several girls over the course of the evening. He would always tell me that he told the various women that he lived with someone. They always replied that I was a lucky woman to be living with someone as funny, attractive and nice as him. At the time I believed every word.

Once he went to meet his friend in a town about eight miles away. He insisted that he would meet me later in our local pub, as I'd arranged to meet my friend Jill that Friday night. I told him not to bother meeting me in the pub. I could have a drink with Jill, get a taxi and meet him back in the house.

"Listen, you go out with your mates. I can go out and about with Jill. There really is no need to meet me in the pub"; I wanted some time with my friend.

"I told you, I'll fucking meet you. I know what a fucking whore you are. You will be giving your phone number to any one who pays you any attention." He glared at me.

"You know that's not true", I answered, "If I wanted to flirt with anyone, which I don't want to do, I'm certainly not going to do so in our local pub"

"I'll be in the pub at eleven o clock. Make sure you

are", he shouted as he went out of the front door.

That then was my plan for the night. I couldn't go anywhere else. I had to be in the pub at the time he said or suffer the consequences later. Eleven o' clock came. I waited at the pub. I waited and waited. I sent him several text messages. I didn't get a reply. I phoned him several times and left several messages on his voice mail that he didn't respond to. I left the pub at twelve thirty. Once I was home I tried texting and phoning him again. There was still no reply. I left another voice mail and went up to bed. He woke me up about three on Saturday morning. Physically woke me up, as he usually did, when he came home from a night out. He would touch me or shake me until I woke up. I asked him where he'd been. He'd been to a very smart dance club, in a town about eight miles away.

"I had to go to this fucking club with my mates. The lads think that I'm too much under the thumb. Anyway they need me there, because they can't pull any women without me", he slurred.

"I know you go where you want to, and I'll never stop you doing that. You should have let me know what your plans were. I was left waiting for you in the pub. Did you tell the lads you'd arranged to meet me?" I asked him.

"Did I fuck? Why should I text you when I'm out with my mates? I see you all the time; we live together for fucks sake. No need for stupid texts so don't make a fuss, I'm home now aren't I? He climbed into bed and went straight to sleep.

No reason why he didn't text me or reply to any of my messages. He just didn't .He did what he

Sour Face

wanted, when he wanted. I did what "HE" wanted. By keeping me waiting at the pub, he knew where I was all evening, and so he was fully in control. Later that morning, he told me that he'd given into peer pressure, "There's nothing wrong with that, so stop flicking your lamps at me, (he meant that I should stop giving him direct eye contact) fucking sour face bitch"

He never gave me an apology for keeping me waiting .He really believed that he had done nothing wrong.

We stood outside the flat waiting for a taxi. We were going into town, to meet friends. It was a warm summer evening.

I was dressed in a silk vest type top and cropped jeans.

A car went past, driven by a young man. He sounded his horn and waved at me smiling as he drove past.

He turned to me scowling," I knew that top was too fucking low, as soon as I saw you wearing it".

"There's nothing wrong with this top. I've worn it lots of times. You have never mentioned that it was too low "

He wasn't listening to me.

"I hate when men toot their car horns at women in the street. The only reason they do it, is because the woman looks like a tart. They behave towards her like they would to any cheap whore, who's selling herself on the street corner".

"I really think you are over reacting"; I was fed up with his negative comments towards my appearance." I have no idea why that man did what he did. Maybe it was someone I knew or knew me. I certainly didn't encourage him in any way".

"If you wear tops that make you look like a tart, you are going to get that type of a reaction from men".

"I personally don't think this makes me look like a tart, but if it makes you happier I'll go and change". I felt that I needed to prove to him I wasn't looking for attention from other men. I wasn't expecting him to say he would like me to change my clothes.

"Yes it would. Thank you, for doing that for me. If the taxi arrives I'll ask it to wait".

I returned from the flat five minutes later in a shirt type top. I made sure that all of the buttons were firmly fastened. I felt that I was dressed for work rather than for an evening out with friends.

"You look great", he said as he hugged me.

"Thank you", I was pleased what I wore met with his approval.

"I just love you so much. You are my woman. I don't want any men looking at your body. I don't want men thinking that you are a cheap tart. You are my smart, elegant woman. "He pulled me towards him and kissed me.

"I'm not prepared to share you with anyone else. I want you for myself, I have never loved anyone the way I love you".

I dismissed the negative thoughts I'd had earlier about having to get changed. I thought I'd over reacted, as I hadn't been in a relationship for a while. I wasn't used to anyone telling me what to do.

I thought he was being so sweet and protective in

Sour Face

an old fashioned way. That was so far from the truth, he wasn't being sweet. He had begun the controlling process.

CHAPTER TWO

I rang Jill. It was now 5am. She answered immediately.
"He's hit me, really hit me. I've left him. I'm standing outside "I sobbed.
"I'll be right down "was her reply. Within a few minutes I was sitting in her lounge, an ice pack on my face. The whole of the right side of my face was now extremely swollen and very red in colour. My cheek area appeared to be raised, and the eye area was puffy, filled with fluid. I looked like a boxer who'd just stepped out of the ring.
"I think you should go to the police", Jill was worried. "What on earth happened?"
"He made a remark about the snooker and I answered him back. He was drunk. I should have had more sense. I should have kept my big mouth shut". I began to cry.
"Well that's hardly a reason to react and hurt you like he has. I still think you should ring the police", Jill was insistent.
"I'll be alright, I'm better now I'm here, I was so upset and I feel shaken up", I replied." I just need time to think".
My mobile ringing interrupted our conversation.
It was him.
"Where the hell are you fucking bitch? I can't believe you sneaked out of the house like a thief in the night. Come back now", he was shouting so loudly, that Jill could hear him from across the room.
"I'm not telling you where I am, you've hurt me, my face is badly swollen". I was trying so hard not

Sour Face

to cry, tears made his behavior worse.

"If you're not back here within half an hour, then I will fucking show you what swollen is. I'll find you wherever you've gone and I'll fucking really hurt you, you cunt, fucking whore. You fucking sour face bitch". I hung up. He rang back and continued to do so at minute intervals for the next twenty minutes. This was the normal pattern of behaviour with him. If he was angry with me, and I wouldn't answer the phone, he would continue to ring over and over until I answered. He would not stop, would not give in until he got what he wanted. That meant me speaking to him.

Jill was very concerned. "Listen I will take you where ever you want to go, I can tell by the look on your face you are thinking of going back. If you do you could end up in hospital, or worse. I've heard how angry he is. Let me take you to the police".

She was right. She knew me so well. I had been thinking of going back. Why? I was ashamed. Ashamed of what my family and friends would say when they found out how he'd been treating me and that I'd let him. I still felt it was my fault that he'd behaved in that way, if I hadn't made that stupid remark, that incident wouldn't have happened.

I can see now how conditioned I was. Two years of constant control had turned me into a puppet; he could pull the strings any time he wanted.

The thought of reporting him to the police filled me with dread. How could I do that to him? How could I betray him? If only I hadn't opened my mouth, said that stupid remark about the dam snooker, then the incident wouldn't have happened. I blamed myself for the entire episode. But I knew that now I had told someone what had happened to me, I had to tell the police. I had to stop him from hurting me. I couldn't do that on my own I needed help.

It took all my strength to say "No, just pass me the phone please mate and I'll ring them".

Jill handed me her phone. "I want you to know, that I think, well we both think you are doing the right thing", she said. Darren nodded in agreement.

My hands were shaking as I dialed the number.

I could hear myself reporting the incident, giving all the details, and answering the questions. It didn't sound like my voice. It didn't feel real. It felt like a dream. At any moment I was going to wake up, I was sure of it. But of course it wasn't a dream.

Half an hour later two uniformed officers arrived at Jill and Darren's house. The process of stopping him hurting me had begun.

Two male police officers arrived to take my statement. They introduced themselves and told me what police station they were from. They then began to explain the procedure that was going to follow.

As part of the current police domestic violence procedures, a risk assessment had to be carried out by the police officers that were interviewing me. This involved a series of routine questions.

Was this the first time he had physically hurt me?
No

Sour Face

Did he have any history of violence towards me? Yes.

Had he ever tried to strangle me? Yes.

Did he have any criminal convictions? Yes, ten years ago. This was now spent.

Did he have any medical conditions? No.

Had he ever raped me? I had to have sex with him when he demanded. He never used physical force, but then he didn't need to. I knew what would happen if I didn't comply.

Did he prevent me from seeing my family and friends, or from going to work? He didn't mind me going to work. He would always cause an argument, which would result in violence if any of my friends or family visited. This would never happen in front of any visitors. Always, when they had gone or were in another room.

Did we have any children under the age of sixteen living with us at the house? No

The interviewing police officer wrote my answers to these questions on a printed form. This risk assessment would be passed on to the domestic violence unit at our local police station. This would determine what physical danger I was actually in, if I continued to be involved in the relationship. It would also highlight what level of police involvement if any, there needed to be.

Before they began to take my statement, they asked me how far I wanted to take the matter.

I looked at them blankly. I was very confused. This was the first time I'd had any involvement with the police.

"I'm really sorry. I don't know what you mean?"

The policeman was calm and professional.

"Do you want to press charges?" He asked.

Did I want to press charges? No. I didn't want to. I wanted to run away and hide .I wanted the entire situation to go away, but it wasn't going to. Darren gave me looks of encouragement. Jill's eyes, told me pressing charges was the right and only choice for me to make. I found myself answering, "Yes, I do want to press charges".

The second policeman took out his notebook and began taking it in turns with his colleague to ask me questions about the attack.

They appeared to be very professional; they asked me the same questions, just phrased differently.

They began the interview by asking me how our relationship was in general.

I explained about his temper and mood swings. I also explained how he displayed these behaviours towards me on a regular basis.

Darren and Jill looked at me in amazement. They couldn't believe that I had kept all the information regarding his behaviours from them.

They then moved on to the events of the day of the attack.

They asked me what his mood had been like prior to going out with his friends. Had we had an argument before he left?

I replied that the last time I had seen him was at eight o'clock that morning. He had appeared settled and in a good mood as he wasn't going to work that day.

We chatted together as I got ready for work. He kissed me goodbye and I told him to have a good time.

Sour Face

He had also rang me at lunchtime to tell me he was waiting for his friends at the train station, and also that he loved me, was missing me and that he would see me back at home later.

They then asked me for full details of the physical attack. I found this task to be extremely difficult. I couldn't answer most of their questions without becoming very distressed.

We stopped several times in order for me to compose myself.

The police officer asked me how he had physically struck me.

Had he punched me, or had he slapped me? Had he used an open or closed hand to hit me? I had no idea. I didn't want to guess. I wanted to be a hundred percent certain that I had told the complete truth regarding the beating. All I knew is that he had hit me four times across the face and had bit me several times on the forearm.

The whole process of giving my statement took over an hour. I felt exhausted by the end of it.

The police officer told me that he knew it wouldn't be easy for me, but would I be prepared to give evidence against him in court if necessary? It was the last thing I wanted to do. Give evidence against someone I cared about. Again the loving supporting, firm look came in my direction from my friends. I found myself also answering yes to that question.

"We have to ask that question. A lot of victims of domestic violence do not continue with the process and will refuse to give evidence against their abuser when the case actually gets to court. A number of victims actually retract their statement. The police will continue with the prosecution process, but the case against the abuser isn't so powerful without the evidence and statement of the victim. "The police officer explained.

I confirmed again that I was prepared to go to court and give evidence against him.

The policemen decided there was enough physical evidence to charge him with assault, arranged police photographers to take pictures of my injuries, and went to arrest him.

The police photographers arrived at Jill and Darren's house. This time it was one male and one female officer. Again they appeared very professional and the whole process took about ten minutes. They photographed my face from different angles they also measured the bite marks on my arm and took several photographs of these injuries. They asked me for all the details of the attack; whilst I gave them my sister arrived. She was distressed by my injuries.

The arresting officers telephoned to inform us that he'd been arrested and was going to be charged with assault. He would be kept in jail for at least two hours. They advised me to go back to my house and get any personal belongings I needed whilst he was in custody.

My sister took me back to the house.

The house was so unnaturally still. My sister accompanied me upstairs.

The bedroom remained how I had left it. The curtains were still drawn; the bedclothes were

Sour Face

pulled back on the side of the bed I usually slept on.

I found myself standing at the side of the bed, staring at the area where the attack had taken place. I found myself crying. My sister comforted me.

"Come on Sis, let's get what you need and leave as soon as possible. Remember, you don't know when you can come back to this house. If I was you I would take everything you need and also anything that is of a sentimental value."

I collected the suitcases from the spare bedroom and began to pack. I don't know what I threw into those suitcases. I was operating on autopilot.

I also took the box that contained all of the details regarding the house purchase and of my recent inheritance. When I looked into the box later that week, I found our joint savings book tucked inside one of the envelopes.

When he was out of custody he rang me to complain what a mess I had left the bedroom in, as I hadn't closed one of the bedside cabinet drawers properly.

After dropping my belongings off at Jill and Darren's house, I agreed to go back with my sister to spend the night at her house. My sister lived about fifty miles away, and the distance would give me some thinking time and physical space from the situation. I was now very emotional, constantly crying, shaking, and feeling sick. Darren and Jill were being as supportive as they could be, but I knew they were finding the situation difficult to deal with. I agreed to return to my friends' house the following day, by then we would know what was happening with him, and I hoped to return to my house after the weekend. My sister had to collect her children from her mother in law's house. She lived in a little village, and in order to reach her house we had to park and walk through a pedestrian area. As I walked through the village people I passed stared at my facial injuries. I felt so ashamed.

My four year old niece looked at me, "Nanny who's that?" she asked as I stood at the door.

"That's your auntie silly", her grandmother replied.
My niece stared at me.

"That's not my auntie", she shouted, and hid behind her mother's legs. I was so upset. My face was so badly injured. My own niece didn't recognise me. Later that evening I discussed the details of my relationship with my sister.

She was shocked and alarmed by the information I gave her.

"You are going to feel upset, you are grieving for what's happened to you and for the end of a relationship, even one as traumatic as the one you've been in".

"But I've been so disloyal. I've betrayed him. I've gone to the police, had him arrested I've put him in jail". I was crying again.

"Now, stop that", my sister's voice was very firm. "Let's get one thing straight. There's only one person who's responsible for putting him in jail. And that's him. It's his behaviour that's resulted in his arrest. You have to realise and believe that".

I listened. I felt my sister was trying to reassure me. That she was trying to make me feel better. I loved my sister for her love and support but I still

Sour Face

felt responsible, a feeling that would remain with me for a very long time.

Throughout the weekend the police kept in regular contact with me. He had pleaded guilty to the charge of common assault. He blamed the incident on the alcohol he had consumed the day before. He claimed to be still drunk when he was arrested.
He had become very emotional when he was shown the photographs of my injuries.
He didn't want bail but had chosen to have legal representation. He had also chosen to remain in custody until his court appearance on Monday morning. Police officers felt he was doing this to appear as if he was punishing himself for his behaviour.
The thought of him staying in a cell all weekend made me feel even sicker than I already felt. I was convinced this was my entire fault. I felt so incredibility guilty about the situation.

Monday morning I rang the police station .I was desperate to find out what was going to happen in court. The desk officer informed me he was due to appear in the local magistrates' court that morning. He'd already been transported from the police cells to the court building. There was no set time for his court case. He was due to appear before the magistrates before twelve o' clock. I then telephoned the court. I wanted to know how I would find out the verdict of the court case. I was anxious. There were lots of questions I wanted answering. Could I go back to my house being the main one? I was gob smacked when the court official informed me she could not give me any information regarding the outcome of the court case. She couldn't tell me due to the data protection act, which protects the accused person. She gave me the number of victim support who she assured me would be able to give me all the information I required. So I rang them. A young man, who was not at all helpful, answered the telephone. He explained the process of giving the victim information. The victim support office fax the court where the hearing is being held, asking them for the verdict of the case. The verdict is then faxed back to victim support, who then informs the victim the following day. This means the victim doesn't know the verdict of the court case until forty-eight hours after the hearing. How frustrating was that? Can you imagine? He told me that the only way I could find out what was happening that day would be if either someone went to court and sat in the public gallery or if I went myself. There was no way I could face him, I wasn't strong enough, and so I couldn't go. I rang my daughter Bernie and asked her if she would attend on my behalf. She agreed and I arranged to meet her after I'd been to see the GP. I had arranged to see the GP on the advice of the police. As the attack happened over the weekend, queuing at the local accident and emergency department in my emotional and physical state was not an option. The purpose of the appointment was to get my injuries examined and recorded by a medical professional. My surgery was excellent, as was my GP, who was so

Sour Face

supportive. I couldn't tell him what had happened without crying. He was so professional, so none judgemental. He told me he was sorry for what had happened to me and that it wasn't my fault. He went on to tell me that no one deserved to be treated the way I had been. No facial bones were broken, there was lots of soft tissue damage, but no permanent damage had been done to my face. Emotionally I was a wreck, and I would be for a long time.

I went from the GP's surgery to the court to meet Bernie, who was waiting for me in the court's reception in tears. He had pleaded guilty to common assault (As he had not broken any of my bones he couldn't be charged with actual bodily harm.)

His solicitor told the court he was hard working with a responsible job. He had a criminal conviction for a similar offence but this was now spent. He hadn't had any further involvement with the police for the past ten years.

The solicitor continued to tell the court that the violence towards me was an isolated incident due to over indulgence in alcohol. He was very remorseful for what he had put me through and had readily pleaded guilty to all charges.

He stood in court, looking a complete wreck. His skin appeared blotchy; there were dark circles underneath his eyes. He was unshaven and remained in the clothes he had worn four days ago.

A discussion took place regarding where he would go when he was released.

The solicitor explained that he owned a house.

The magistrates then released him back to my home.

Due to this guilty plea he had been ordered to pay me £500 compensation.

The magistrates decided he needed help to manage his anger and advised that he had a chat with a RMN about alcohol misuse before he left the court. He was then released to go back to my home. I couldn't go back there so I was left lodging at Darren and Jill's house. The £500 compensation he had been ordered to pay me came out of our joint bank account that I contributed the majority of the money to. (I actually earned twice as much as he did.) No one bothered to ask if the bank account was in joint names. All the court was interested in was if he had a job and could he afford to pay £500. Bernie was so upset if he hadn't paid his television licence he would have had a prison sentence. He had injured me so badly that my own niece didn't recognise me. I paid myself compensation and on top of that, in order to maintain my personal safety, I was unable to return to my own home. It seemed and still does seem absolutely ridiculous. But that was the court's decision, which was final, and I couldn't do a thing about it.

I have obtained the common assault sentence guidelines issued to magistrates. The starting point for sentencing is a community penalty; the seriousness of the offence including "the impact on the victim" must be taken into account, as should relevant previous convictions. If the offender offers a "timely guilty plea", a reduction in the sentence should be considered. This is obviously what happened in my case.

Domestic violence is the only crime where the victim gets punished twice: once by the perpetrator and secondly by the "system".

The victim has lost everything, their home and their possessions. (I left my home with just my personal possessions). Yet society thinks this is acceptable, provide a refuge for women with children, the rest of the victims go and find somewhere else to live, they can start again no matter how old they are. They are safe that's all that matters. The abuser can return to the family home their lives unaffected by the situation.

Is this a fair system to have operating in a civilised 21st century society?

Domestic violence accounts for 16% of all violent crimes. (Nicholas, Povey and Walker 2004). Weapons are less likely to be used but victims are more likely to be injured. On average a woman is beaten thirty five times before she will report the abuser to the police. (Jaffe 1986). These are common research facts I have come across many times in articles on abuse in various women's magazines. Given these facts, that domestic violence is what it says, violence towards another human being, I strongly believe that the starting point for all common assaults should be greater than a community penalty. He thought he was going to jail for three months, due to my injuries and his previous criminal record. He was surprised to be allowed "off with a fucking fine".

I did write to the local magistrate's court voicing

my concerns. I felt very let down by them. Their verdict made me feel that I'd been punished twice, once by him and then by them. I felt that somewhere in the magistrates training, issues of compensation orders when a couple lived together and had a joint account should be raised. Effectively he had beaten me up, paid me compensation and that was the matter resolved. No other punishment was deemed to be necessary. They did reply to my letter, stating that the decision was final and that there was no one else I could complain to. Six months later, a local magistrate, informed me that magistrates in our borough are no longer allowed to issue compensation orders from joint accounts. Did my letter have anything to do with that change of policy? I hope so, even if it just raised awareness of the issue, it was worth writing. I didn't want to write the letter. It would have much easier to sit back and accept their decision. But I knew, deep inside of me, that their decision was very wrong. How will crazy unfair rules be changed if no one makes the effort to challenge them?

There appears to be no consistency by magistrates regarding the sentencing of domestic violence perpetrators.

I have sat in the public galleries of my local magistrates courts observing various domestic violence cases. I have seen such diversity in the punishment given to abusers. It appears to depend on the individual magistrates and will differ greatly between courts. Even though the courts are located a few miles from each other and operated by the same council.

Sour Face

Again, this is an area that needs to be addressed. Surely consistency in dealing with the consequences of domestic violence is the way forward in handling the punishments for domestic abusers. Otherwise the whole criminal justice system appears to be a big joke and victims will be even more reluctant to come forward and report what is happening to them.

CHAPTER THREE

What was he like this man? What was it about him that attracted women to him?

He was tall, over six feet in height, large built, not fat, weighing about fifteen stone. He had a broad chest, medium waist, and long muscular tanned legs that he liked to show off at any opportunity. He wore shorts or calf length trousers with top of the range trainers whenever he wasn't at work. He told me he had very pretty hands for a man and liked to keep his nails short, spending a lot of time filing them to a smooth shape with an emery board.

He was very vain. He liked to stand in front of the mirror naked, posing, admiring himself from all different angles.

He had a very attractive face. Large blue grey coloured eyes, clear olive skin, even white teeth (he would walk around the house brushing them with a special whitening toothpaste purchased off the internet, for long periods of time), and full lips. He had a small thin strip of facial hair stretching from his bottom lip to his chin. He would moisturize his face with a male face cream product. He liked to use expensive designer aftershaves, and would drown himself in the pungent heady smell of his favorite.

He had collar length wavy black hair, which was cut into a bob type style. He would ware it in a ponytail, when we were staying at home, or when working out in the gym. He would spend a lot of money on quality hair care products such as shampoo and conditioner and wax; he would then

Sour Face

spend a lot of time "fixing his hair".

His going out or clubbing clothes' as he liked to call them were expensive; he liked to wear designer labeled shirts, proper going out shirts with long sleeves and collars.

His jackets were also expensive from the up market high street shops. The same applied to his socks. He would get very upset if a hole appeared in one of them. When we lived together he would blame me for it, saying it was my fault for not cutting his toenails for him, because he hated doing it himself.

He would only wear designer jeans, that were well cut and showed his bottom to its full potential. He was very proud of his bum, and would exercise to keep it pert.

He spoke with a clear Gloucestershire accent. This was strange as he wasn't from that part of the country. He was a very good communicator articulate with a base knowledge in many subjects.

He loved to read, a good knowledge of books and literature was a requirement of his job, but he had a passion for books of any kind. He had a very detailed knowledge of modern books and contemporary authors. He would talk for hours on this subject whether you wanted to take part in the conversation or not.

He smiled a lot, gave lots of eye contact when chatting, and appeared charming and confident with women. He would talk to a woman and make her feel like she was the only woman in the world. He would pay her compliments, very subtle compliments, and use open body language. He would later claim he had slept with over a hundred women, who all confirmed he was an excellent lover.

He loved appearing as the nice guy in public. The guy all his mates wanted to be like. He would pretend to be witty when out with the boys, but really he didn't have a sense of humour. If someone made a witty remark about him, or exchanged banter with him he'd smile and laugh in the right places, but when we were alone he would question me about it. What did they really mean? Were they humiliating him? He was very paranoid. I would always reply with "I have no idea, ask them." But he never did.

I remember the first time I teased him. He bit my head off "What do you mean by that", he yelled. It took at least an hour to explain that I was just teasing him, pulling his leg. He just looked at me and smiled he thought I was rather funny. That was at the beginning of the relationship. Later he would say he hated my sarcastic sour face comments.

He'd had a turbulent childhood. His mother became pregnant with him at sixteen and married a Scottish man who was in the royal navy. They spent his early years living in the naval bases in the south west of England where his sibling was born. He was told as a child that the man he called" dad" was not his biological father. His "dad "was physically abusive towards him when he was a child, but not towards his sibling. When he was physically aggressive to me his accent would change. He would verbally abuse me with a

Sour Face

Scottish accent. He hated the way his "dad" had treated him when he was a child,

"He was a fucking arsehole. Fucking bully the way he would beat me for nothing. He would just come back from work in a bad mood and he would take it out of me. He knocked me black and blue, but the fucking bastard was dead sly. He'd mark me in places where the bruises didn't show."

I have researched the link between abused children growing up to become abusers themselves. I have found the following information.

A man may have witnessed his father abusing his mother or his parents may have abused him, so it may not seem wrong to him, but normal. (Carr and Van Deusen 2002)

This research is inconclusive, experiencing or witnessing aggression my also lead to a hatred of violence and this results in the man growing up determined not to be an abuser. (Mullender 1996). My personal view is that someone chooses to be abusive.

His mother and "dad" had a stormy relationship; they were both physically aggressive towards each other on a regular basis.

His mother took him and his sibling to the local fun fair. On returning she left them with a neighbour, on the pretence of going to collect some milk, from the nearby shops. She never came back. She didn't contact him or any of her family until ten years later.

His "dad" didn't want anything to do with him after his mother had left. He began to make plans to have him placed in the care of the local social services department.

His auntie (She was in fact his mother's aunt) heard of his dad's plans and stepped in. She wanted to prevent him from going into care, as she was certain that his mother would come back for him at some stage. She applied successfully to be his legal guardian and arranged for him to go and live with her. His dad decided to leave the area and took his sibling to live in Scotland. He never heard from either one of them again.

His auntie, a widow, was a woman who had worked hard during her life- time. She had ten children and numerous grand children. She was the head of the family and was always there to help her family in any way she could. She doted on him, spoilt him, and told him constantly how special he was. She gave him everything he asked for, paying for his driving lessons and buying him his first car. She over compensated with material things to make up for her niece, his mother abandoning him.

She would tell him how attractive he was. She also told him that when he was older he would have a very attractive partner. This person would be really special. His auntie felt he deserved someone really special because he was a really wonderful person. And that person would look after him and do everything for him. That is what he deserved. This treatment continued into his adult life. She felt that I did not have the required beauty queen looks that her nephew's girl friend should have. I did however have a fairly well paid job and was also a good cook. She felt these were plus factor and gave our relationship her blessing.

Sour Face

When we went to visit her he would drop hints about items that he needed, she would always get these for him and give them to him the next time we went to see her. His auntie was a pensioner, and I felt bad that she was spending her money on items for him that he could easily buy for him self. We were both working full time and money was not an issue for us. I would tell her that she needed to keep her money to buy items for herself that no matter what he told her we were fine for money. She didn't listen to me. She bought him a designer suit that cost over six hundred pounds. He strutted around the house wearing it, telling me what good quality material it was made of. It was a very nice suit. In my opinion it seemed like a lot of money to take from an old lady. I told him so. "That's just the way she is. She likes getting me stuff I need." When I arranged for a mobile hairdresser to visit her at her home and I paid for it, he was not happy.

"Why are you spending our fucking money for? My aunt has got plenty of her own money. She doesn't need ours," he yelled.

"She's good to you, and it's nice to do things for other people. She deserves spoiling once in a while", I replied,

"As long as you realise you can't fucking spend and save money. I'm fed up with your fucking reckless spending".

His auntie was delighted with the pampering she received. She thanked him profusely. He took the thanks and praise. He thought he was great. His auntie's constant praise built up his ego. When we were alone, he told me "We've paid for her hair once. Don't get making any more appointments. She's got enough money in the bank to pay for herself." That was the first and last hair dressing appointment his auntie ever received.

His family had no respect for each other. They swore at each other constantly. Even his Auntie swore, real strong swear words. I found if very surprising to hear a seventy year old woman say "fuck" in normal every day conversations.
Out of the blue, his mother returned to the area. She had had no contact with him for ten years.
His mother had moved to mainland Spain where she met and married her current husband, whilst working in a British bar. She did have a dependency on alcohol and remained a heavy drinker, on her return to England.
His mother went on to have four children with her second husband, his half siblings. They lived about ten miles away and he was a regular visitor to his mother's home.
 He and his mother had a strange relationship. He didn't like her but felt that he should have a relationship with her because "you only have one mother". I couldn't understand this need to be involved with a Mother that, one, you didn't need and two you didn't like. His auntie encouraged the relationship between him and his mother.
His mother was in her late forties, small in height about five feet tall, with very short greying, blonde hair. Her skin was red and blotchy, she never wore make up, or deodorant and would smell of body odour. Her four front teeth were missing, making her appear older than her years. Her

Sour Face

clothing was always casual consisting of badly fitting tracksuits and sweatshirts. She never wore a bra, and her breasts would swing around freely in her clothes. She was overweight with an obvious "beer belly", and was a chain smoker of roll ups. Her house was always full of cigarette smoke. She appeared fairly intelligent, but was lazy. She didn't work, choosing instead to live off state benefits, her philosophy being "why struggle working with four kids when you can get more money staying at home. Let the government pay for my rent, they've got more money than me".

She'd call him her baby, whenever we visited, and would wait on him hand and foot.

She often told me that she didn't have a mother son relationship with him. In her opinion theirs was more a brother and sister relationship. That's the way she saw the situation. He didn't view it like that at all. He wanted her to be a mother to him, and when she wasn't, when she failed him and let him down, because she didn't see him as a son, he would take it out on me. She found him very difficult to deal with. She ignored his bizarre behaviours. It was easier to dip in and out of his life and not take any parental responsibility for the monster she had helped to create.

When he was in custody, I rang her. All I could think about was him. That he would need somebody to be there for him. He would need some personal items taking to the police station, as he was to remain in jail for two days.

The arresting officers asked me if I wanted to take him some belongings to the police station.

Apparently in their experience it's extremely common for victims to arrive at the police station with various items of clothing and food for their abuser. The victim still feels the need to look after the abuser. This is a classic feature of traumatic bonding.

This was his choice to remain in jail. He'd been offered bail but refused to accept it. He told me later that he didn't need "fucking anybody. I've got me. That's all I need. I won't let me down like every fucker else does".

She panicked at the news. She was upset that he'd been arrested, but was more upset that she'd been given information that she needed to action. I rang her later, to arrange for her to collect some of his belongings, from my house. She told me he'd refused to speak to her when she rang the police station, so she wasn't going to see him or take him any things, as it would upset her if he shouted at her. She didn't want to fall out with him. She was ashamed and scared of him. I can see that so clearly now. She couldn't cope with him. The responsibility of being his mother was too much for her to cope with. To be fair she couldn't really cope with life in general.

When we first met, he told me he'd been divorced for six years.

"I was working at the supermarket, fucking stacking shelves. I hated it, but it gave me my beer money for the weekend."

She worked as a cashier.

"She was fucking gorgeous, long red hair, great body. She was older than me just the way I like my women". He looked thoughtful. "She was married but hated her husband. She had wanted to leave him for a long time. I really loved her and she felt the same about me. So we moved in together. I carried on working in that fucking shit hole of a supermarket for fucking peanuts".

I got used to him giving me several versions of the same story. He told so many lies he forgot what he had told me. They married as soon as her divorce came through.

From his account the marriage was aggressive with them both being violent to each other.

"She had a real bad fucking temper. It's true what they say about red heads. She was really fiery. I couldn't open my mouth without her fucking reacting."

He has a scar on the outer aspect of his left leg, where his wife allegedly cut him with a kitchen knife during an argument .A year after they were married they had a child. He stayed with his wife until the baby was six months old. He couldn't cope being a dad and living on the bread line.

"We had fucking nothing. Not even a pot to piss in. She had to give up work to look after the kid, didn't even want to go back to work part time. We had to survive on my fucking wages. We had to have the cheapest of everything; thank god I had a staff discount on the bits of shopping I bought from there. It didn't bother her. All she wanted was kids. How can you bring up kids when you haven't got enough money for yourself? I didn't get a fucking look in once the kid was born. I couldn't live like that. Fucking made me depressed".

He left his marriage returning to live with his auntie, who persuaded him to go back to his wife for the sake of the child.

Ten months later he went back to his wife to find she was now pregnant with a previous partner's child. The relationship was obviously over and he returned to his auntie's house.

He hadn't seen his child since it was one year old because" I can't be a fucking part time dad. Let them bring it up".

"Any way I'm not paying for some kid that I do not fucking see".

"If you sorted out maintenance you would get chance to see the child", I encouraged him, "with both of our wages we can afford it".

"No fucking way. I'm not paying for some little bastard that I get to see once a week. I've already told you that. I'll divorce her when it's eighteen, then I won't have to pay a penny, they'll be an adult".

I was horrified.

"Hang on a minute, you told me you were divorced six years ago. You mean you're still married?"

"We haven't been together for six years. Stop being a jealous cunt. I'm not getting a divorce just to please you. Nobody tells me what to do".

"I'm not jealous, just as mad as hell with you for lying to me. I've just found out you're not divorced and have no intention of becoming divorced. I don't understand it", I was very angry with him.

"You're not meant to understand anything, just accept that's the way it is", was his answer.

He bought me an engagement ring for my birthday. It was paid for out of our joint account.

"It has a one carat diamond. I got it off one of my mates whose brother is in the jewellery trade. It

Sour Face

cost £300. Guess how much it retails for?" He asked me.

I had no idea. "It would cost over a thousand pounds if you bought it from a shop. Made a great saving" was his reply.

I never wanted that ring. Being engaged to him was a complete sham.

"Now you've got the ring, there's no need to make a fuss". He said to me. "Don't get asking people round to celebrate or anything. All they will do is want to know our business. They'll ask lots of questions like have we set a fucking wedding date. We both know that that can't happen, because I need to stay married. We can look at the situation again in ten years. Don't look at me with that sour face; getting married is just a fucking piece of paper any way".

"If you feel like that why bother getting engaged?" I asked him.

"Well, because I want to. I want the outside world to look at us and see a respectable committed couple. We've been together long enough, the time is right. It doesn't mean that we're getting married dim wit. Just means you get a nice ring. You are so old fashioned at times. I can't believe that you think, receiving an engagement ring means that we'll be getting married. You are so fucking prim, you really make me laugh"

Why be engaged when he would never really commit to me, when all he wanted was to remain married to someone else?

When our relationship ended, His mother told me that she didn't condone his aggressive behaviour.

She also said that she felt I shouldn't have made a fuss and reported the incident to the police. Again she couldn't or wouldn't face up to the reality of what he was really like.

She made me promise not to tell his auntie the reason why we'd split up, she didn't want her upset at the "thought of him getting into trouble again. I don't want the shock to cause her to have a further stroke. She's not been well recently"
So I didn't tell her.

I saw his auntie during the week that followed the physical attack, whilst I was shopping. My facial injuries were still very evident. I felt so ashamed, so completely responsible for any hurt or upset I had caused his auntie by reporting his abuse to the police.

I hid in one of the food aisles until she left the store.

When we spilt up, his mother contacted me to tell me he wanted half of the money we had in a joint savings account. This account held the remainder of my inheritance, but it was in joint names and legally half of the money belonged to him. She kept on telling me it was HIS money and I needed to hand it over to him because he needed it. I could have choked her. She made me so very angry. When he was working abroad he left several items of expensive jewellery with her for safe keeping. She sold these items to fund a holiday. She never said she was sorry or paid the money back to him. This was the woman he wanted a mother son relationship with. She didn't think twice about stealing from her own son. I couldn't understand why he'd want a person like this in his life, someone who so obviously didn't care for him or about him. He would always repeat his parrot fashion answer "You only get one mother and you need to make it work". But he really didn't like her one bit. He would always criticise her and her life style behind her back, but never to her face. Yet he would never tire of letting me know his negative feelings about me. I feel that he took out the intense dislike he had for his mother on our relationship. Yet he still insisted on maintaining it.

When I left him, she told everyone who would listen that the relationship had ended because I had taken all of HIS money from our joint account and left him with nothing. I wish I had done that now. That was a case of when doing the right thing wasn't the right thing to do, because morally that money didn't belong to him. She failed to mention the severe facial injuries and two years of abuse he had subjected me to. She continues to protect him. She needs to realise that she does have a responsibility for the way her son behaves. I say this because if we know any information that can help another human being, we need to pass this on. She knows what he has done, what he is capable of. (She told me to get a court order to prevent him from harming me to that extent again She felt that he shouldn't be in a "real" relationship with a woman.

She told me "he should leave all women alone. He can't help the way he is. He should just have someone for sex now and again. He needs to live on his own. If he's by his self, no woman can get him into trouble")

All his relationships had ended very badly because he couldn't cope .She never told him that. She feared his reaction. The aggression he has displayed towards women has intensified with each relationship he has had. His mother has a moral duty to tell his next girl friend this information. It would then be up to her what she chooses to do. I would tell her to run as fast as she could in the opposite direction.

CHAPTER FOUR

People reading this will ask the question "Why would she stay with someone who treated her so badly"? This question implies that it was my responsibility to end his abuse. There was something wrong with me for tolerating it. If a woman leaves the abuser will he stop abusing forever? If he continues to abuse will it be his next victim fault that the abuse has happened again, or will society finally stand up and say" how does he keep getting away with abusing women"? Maybe if society stops blaming the women for tolerating the abuse punishes the abuser more and takes time to try and understand the psychology of domestic abuse more women would have the courage and support to leave the relationship.

Women in general can be very critical of other women. The following quotes are from everyday conversations about domestic violence that I have had with women.

"It's her own fault if she allows herself to be treated in a violent way".

"Domestic violence only happens to weak people".

"If any man hit me I'd wait until he was asleep and hit him back with a baseball bat. I would never allow myself to be abused".

"Women stay in abusive situations because they enjoy the drama of the situation".

"If the woman didn't enjoy being abused they would leave."

"Women who get involved with domestic abusers are usually alcoholics or drug addicts".

Stark and Flitcraft (1996) state that women who experience domestic violence are fifteen more times more likely to be alcohol dependent and nine times more likely to have an addiction to drugs.

I have spoken to various recovering victims of domestic violence. Some of them did drink on a regular basis during the abusive relationship. None of them had been heavy drinkers before this. Once the relationship had finished, none of them continued to drink on a regular basis. The alcohol gave them a short time of escape from the abuse. On a personal note, I could not have survived that turbulent time without my regular Friday evenings out. I have been unable to find any current research to challenge the findings of stark.

It's interesting to note that all of the information I have looked at regarding the theories surrounding domestic violence has been written and is available to professionals, such as probation officers and health visitors. Strange that the person who collated this information didn't think it was necessary to provide it in a format that was accessible and easy to understand for the victim.

It appears to me that the people responsible for collating this information believe in the stereotypical victim. Uneducated, not very intelligent, an alcoholic or drug addict.

They have made the assumption that; victims need information from the professionals, as the victim can't understand such complicated information on their own.

Sour Face

Not all victims come into contact with these professionals. I certainly didn't.
What's the good of giving the reasons for domestic violence exclusively to health professionals? Shouldn't society be sharing all this information with the victim, who is so desperately trying to understand what's happening to them?
We have all heard the phrase that knowledge is power.
A reason for not passing on knowledge to the victim could be that some organisations and professionals want to keep the power. This is my personal opinion.
Victims should be empowered. This will only happen when they are given all the information that is available about domestic abuse. Not just practical information. Of course this information is both important and essential. But in order to make the transition from victim to survivor, we need to make sense of what has happened to us emotionally. A victim can't do that with out being given all of the facts and theories surrounding domestic abuse.

I've researched the subject of domestic abuse extensively to try to make sense of what happened to me. Victims of repeated domestic violence go through various psychological stages in order to adapt to what's happening to them.
 Symonds in 1980, states that the response to victimisation has four stages.

Straight after the attack, the victim goes through the stage of felling shocked, of disbelief or goes into denial. I'd make excuses for his behaviour; He couldn't help losing his temper. He didn't mean to hit me at all he just lost control.

When the victim realises what's happening to them they enter stage two, Symonds refers to this as "frozen fright". The victim has strong feelings of being isolated and of being powerless. This can result in the victim separating their mind from their body during a physical attack.

In stage three the victim "keeps busy" as a delayed coping response to the violence. I always had plenty of jobs to do. He'd make sure of that. But I would find housework to do to occupy my mind, rather than sit with him and think about how badly he'd treated me.

In the fourth stage the victim looses their ability to live as an adult and in order to cope with the situation returns to behaviours they learnt as a child, such as obedience and submission. I would do whatever he wanted, always gave in to his demands, however inappropriate they were, and generally let him have his own way with everything. If this stage continues over a period of time the victim may begin to "identify with the perpetrator", in order to avoid their own sense of helplessness, (Domestic violence a practitioner's portfolio).

This can be explained further by the following quote,

"The abuser becomes not only the source of pain

and abuse but also the protector, as they are not only the person being abusive but also the only person who can prevent the violence. This increases the victim's dependency on him" (Hidden hurt web site 2007).

In 1979 Walker describes a condition called the battered woman syndrome, which is a result of being exposed to a relationship where there is irregular abuse. Walker refers to all types of domestic abuse as battering, not just physical abuse.

The victim suffers symptoms such as flashbacks and anxiety.

There are other symptoms present:

The victim thinks that the abuser is misunderstood or that'll he will change.

The victim feels they can manage the abusers behaviour, including episodes of aggression.

The victims suppress their own anger.

I identify with all of these symptoms described above, as the accounts of his behaviour demonstrate. Some of the women I have spoken to who have been in abusive relationships for a period of time, tell of feelings identical to those expressed by Walker. Of course at the time, we didn't know these feelings were symptoms. If anyone had suggested this to me at that time, I would have told him or her in no uncertain terms that they were stupid. These symptoms are the victim's way of coping with the situation they find themselves in.

On the occasions that I did answer him back I was made to regret it. This would result in me being grabbed by the neck and dragged into the corner of the room. He usually pinned me behind the door in the kitchen or in the hallway. He would hold me there by my neck, holding his face very close to mine, so I could feel his breath across my chin. He would then shout in my face. His words were pronounced; spit falling from his mouth:" Lazy. You are a stupid sour face bitch. Who do you think you are to answer me back? You're here to do as you are fucking told. You're not at fucking work now. You can't talk to me like that…cunt…whore…fucking bitch."

He also liked to head butt me. He would put his head against mine whilst I was still in the corner of the room, spit abusive words at me, and then move his head so that my head was knocked sharply by his. He would do this several times. He did this once when my children (Bernie and Matt), came to our house for a meal. They were in the sitting room. He came home from work into to kitchen to find out what I was making for tea. He didn't like me making a fuss when my children came to visit. Rather he didn't want me to spend money on any extra shopping. He also didn't like me laying the table, he wanted us all to eat off our laps, the fact we only had two trays didn't matter.
"Who do you think you are laying the table like the fucking queen? Stop pretending to be something you're not. All you are is a stupid bitch from a fucking council estate. I can't believe you're making all this fuss over your precious kids". So I

Sour Face

used up all the ingredients I had already in the house. He looked at the food in disgust.

" I'm not eating that shit. Why do you always cook such crap?"

"It's not crap. You like this tea, you told me the last time I cooked it. You don't want me to spend any extra money when Matt and Bernie come to tea. It was the only dish I could think of making that was inexpensive ", I replied

He wasn't listening.

"Who the fuck, do you think you're talking to bitch? I'm sick of telling you to stop fucking answering back". He grabbed me by the neck, pinned me in the corner of the kitchen, and head butted me. I saw stars.

" Do you think that I care your stupid spoilt kids are in the next room? I won't let you disrespect me. Go on call them. See if I care".

Of course I didn't shout for them to help me. He knew I wouldn't. He had such control over me. He strode into the sitting room chatting with Matt and Bernie, being the "nice guy", leaving me to compose myself in the kitchen.

Another time they were due to visit me. Matt came to the front door and I had to turn him away. I hated myself for doing it but I had no choice. We'd had a row. Well, that's a contradiction. He'd call it a row, but I wasn't allowed to say anything, just listen to him shouting at me. I couldn't answer him back. He didn't allow it. He would stop me responding verbally by grabbing my chin tight, and squeezing my mouth shut with his thumb and index finger. I can't remember what the argument was about. If anyone had upset him at work, he would come home in a foul mood. He'd then take it out on me. He would grab my neck, and throw things at me. The television controls were his favourite. They really hurt when they make contact with you. He threw everything with force, keys slippers, and books. When Matt knocked on the door, I was crying. He'd grabbed my neck and thrown various items at me, one after the other. I just told Matt we were having a row and I was really sorry, but didn't think it was fair to let him in. He seemed a little surprised, but being the nice lad he is, told me not to worry and left. I then text Bernie and told her the same. She was not a bit happy with me turning Matt away. That was very understandable. How could I let them in when he'd treated me in that way? I couldn't pretend in front of them that everything was all right.

Looking back, I can see a pattern. He would always cause an argument or behave abusively towards me when we expecting visitors, especially when the children visited me. He would constantly find fault with my friends and family, giving these faults as valid reasons why he didn't want them to visit. He liked the two of us to be alone together all the time when we were in the house. He couldn't understand why I'd want to have any one else in my life but him.

Domestic abusers isolate their victims in this way as it increases the control they have over their victim. I became reliant on him for all of my social needs; only going out with him, only going where he wanted me to go and only going out with friends he thought were socially acceptable.

I have also found that abusers usually have very

intense relationships. These usually move at a very quick pace, with a whirlwind courtship resulting in a long-term commitment within a few months. This could be either in the form of living together or marriage. Research states that this is probably due to the perpetrator's coercion of the victim.

During my research I have found several definitions of domestic violence. Greater London Domestic Violence Strategy in 2001 defined domestic violence as:"the misuse of power and the exercise of control by one adult person, usually a man, over another adult, usually a woman, within the context of an intimate relationship. Such abuse may manifest itself in a variety of ways including physical violence, emotional or psychological abuse, sexual violence and abuse, financial control and abuse and the imposition of social isolation or movement deprivation." This definition explains all of the abuse I personally experienced during our relationship.

The above definition lists the types of abuse experienced by victims. Seldom do you find only one type of abuse displayed by a perpetrator. When one type of abuse is present this is usually accompanied by another form of abuse.

It's important for readers to remember that domestic abuse is not an uncommon problem in our society. It is though unusual to find this problem admitted and freely discussed by its victims. My research has led me to believe that the reasons for this could be the feelings of shame and responsibility that the victim experiences. Due to these feelings of responsibility the victim makes allowances and excuses for the abusers behaviour.

I would not have described the behaviours he displayed towards me as domestic violence or abuse, whilst I was living the relationship. This was just the way he was, he couldn't express his feelings any other way, he had a very quick temper, but it wasn't his fault he couldn't control it.

Physical abuse is the most obvious type of domestic violence. Even the smallest of pushes during a heated argument, when both parties are angry at each other, is in fact physical abuse. The victim should not make any allowances for the abuser's behaviour. The abuser has chosen to be violent towards the victim. Research has shown that once physical violence has begun it will increase in frequency and severity.

Verbal abuse is also a very obvious form of abuse. It includes shouting, swearing, insulting, and making fun of the victim. The abuser will usually blame the victim for this behaviour. "Well if you didn't fucking wind me up, I wouldn't have to shout at you". Was a common phrase he would use to justify the behaviour he displayed towards me.

Sexual abuse is defined as any sexual act that takes place without the full consent of both parties. It is important to remember that it's not just physical force that is used in domestic violence. Coercion is commonly used in this type of abuse. Sexual abuse can also include forcing sex or taking part in any sex acts when the victim is tired or not feeling well. Again this isn't necessarily by the use of physical force. I have had sex with him

Sour Face

on a number of occasions when I have had a bad cold and when I've been exhausted. It was the last thing I wanted to be doing. All I really wanted was to sleep. He would nag and torment me with the threat of sleeping with someone else if I refused to have sex with him. It was just easier to let him have his own way.

Other victims have told me they have had sex with their partners when they haven't wanted to as the abuser has threatened aggression towards their children or pets.

Most perpetrators also display bouts of excessive jealously.

He liked to check my mobile phone, taking it out of my handbag checking the call and message history. If I objected to this invasion of my privacy, he would accuse me of having a reason to hide my phone from him. Of course in order to prove my innocence I would accept this screening of my phone calls.

He would also check my e-mails and open any post that arrived addressed to me.

He would boast about his sexual conquests as part of the "no secrets" pact we had made at the beginning of our relationship. I was expected to sit there and listen to all of the details of the relationships, including all of the sexual details, without showing any emotion. If I did show any emotion this would indicate to him that I was jealous. He "hated fucking jealous women". This would give him the excuse he needed to be abusive towards me. He would compare his sex life with each ex girlfriend to our sex life. Of course I didn't live up to any of them. They were all sex goddesses.

He mentioned one whom he met at work with great fondness.

He turned and asked me if I had ever gone out with anyone at work.

"No. That would be too difficult to manage if anything went wrong in the relationship. I was asked out by one of the male nurses on a unit once, but I refused. We agreed to stay friends".

"Did you fancy him", he asked me.

"Yes, he was attractive, but I liked him. I didn't want to complicate our friendship", I replied.

"Fucking Whore!" he yelled as he leapt towards me, grabbing my neck and slamming me against the kitchen wall.

He later apologised for his behaviour stating "I'm sorry for grabbing you, but it was your fault for telling me about that man. I just get so jealous."

The fact that I had actually answered a question he had asked me and that he expected me to answer was irrelevant.

I accepted his apology but never told him any further details of any of my previous relationships.

Emotional or psychological abuse is a very subtle form of domestic abuse. The victim usually doesn't realise that they are actually being abused. I certainly didn't. I just thought he was in a bad mood, due to being stressed at work, or being tired. When used over a period of time emotional abuse can wear the victim down, undermining the victim's confidence so much that they become willing to take responsibility for the abusers behaviour.

Sour Face

I recognised that he had emotional problems. I thought being abandoned by his mother and abused by his "dad" were the reasons behind it. If I could prove to him that I wasn't going to leave him, no matter what he did to me, then I thought he would realise I loved him, and he would stop the abuse.

Of course, I now know that this would never be the case.

In his book the abusive personality, Donald Dutton describes the research he'd carried out on physically aggressive perpetrators. Dutton describes a behaviour that flows from one phase to another, leading to" a repetitive form of personality." One of the key features of this was that the abuser "experienced repeated dissatisfaction with whom ever they were attached to". The perpetrators behaviour changed in a predictable way over time. He also discovered that these perpetrators have a split between their public and private selves.

The extensive research I have carried out has shown me that whilst in a relationship, domestic abusers will never stop abusing their victims. Due to the traumatic bonding that has taken place; the victim will continue to tolerate this behaviour.

I have been thinking about his face, his expressions when he was being abusive. His face would change. I have heard it said about people but I really thought it was an exaggeration until I met him. His eyes would bulge in his face. He would stare expression fixed, unblinking, he kept his eyes firmly fixed on me. I had to maintain eye contact with him. He would make sure of this by pulling my hair with both of his hands, bringing my eye line in line with his. There would be such a look of hate, and contempt in his eyes. His forehead would be burrowed. His mouth twisted in cruel lines. His body language was intrusive. He would puff out his chest and stand really tall, showing his full height. He stood a foot taller in height than me. He would stand in my own personal space. If I took one step backwards, he would take one step towards me. He would stop this once I'd reached the corner of the room. It came to a point where I would put myself in to the corner of a room. It felt that was where I should be. If I were in the corner already, there would be no need for him to drag me there. Once he was pacing towards me I knew I was going to be abused physically. Going to the corner would make it happen quicker. Get it over with. Towards the end of our relationship, he'd pull me out of the corner and drag me anywhere else and pin me against any wall, always by my neck. I can see that he'd do that to get the control back. When I was in the corner, I could protect my face with my hands and try to push his hands away, as I had my back against the wall, I had firm footing which helped me keep my balance. When you're being dragged around your neck, you're falling all over the place as you're off balance. You have no chance of defending yourself.

He would also grab me by the hair. On numerous occasions he pulled me up stairs by my hair. He would hold my hair in both hands and pull my head backwards so my neck was at an angle. I always felt that I was going to fall. He would grab

Sour Face

my neck with both hands and push me into the corner of a room. Again I was always walking backwards. I would try to push his hands away from my neck but he would just tighten his grip. He would never abuse me in front of a window or in any part of a room that could be observed through the window. He would always insist that any curtains we brought for the house were fully lined. He wanted to protect his privacy. This was the reason he gave for his behaviour, and didn't want anyone looking in through the windows. He would pull me from view by my hair and then drag me into the corner of the room.

When I was in the corner he would just hold me there. He would either shout words of abuse or spit in my face. He would also like to grab my neck and push me around the house. He did this on a daily basis during the last six months of our relationship. The worst time would be when he decided to attack me before I went to work. I would get out of the bed after him. He would always go downstairs and make the drinks, coffee for me, and a pot of tea for him. This was his daily domestic duty (only during work days, Monday to Friday). He'd bring the coffee upstairs; to make sure I was up out of the bed. He would then return to the sitting room where he would drink the whole pot of tea and watch the news until half past seven. By that time he'd expect me to be fully ready for work and in the kitchen, so I could make him another cup of tea (I had to do this as he'd made me a drink in the morning and it was only fair that I made him one in return). I also had to put the cereal in the bowl, with just the right amount of milk. Too much and he complain. It would have to be thrown away, and I'd begin again. If I weren't downstairs on time, he'd come into the bedroom to look for me. He begin to be verbally abusive

"What have you been fucking doing? Have you been preening yourself? You're so fucking vain. Who do you think wants to look at you when you're so old and ugly? Look at you staring at me with your fucking sour face. Don't you flick your lamps at me you fucking cunt. You're such a grumpy nasty cunt in the morning. Now you're going to make late for fucking work"

I didn't answer him back. It was pointless. Nothing would stop him when he'd got to this stage of anger. He would grab my neck, drag me across the bedroom to the doorway, then he'd let me go so I'd stumble backwards, and lose my balance. Once I reached the kitchen, he'd grab my neck again.

"You've always got to start haven't you, you sour face cunt. You always have got to upset me before I go to work".

I used to carry on as much as I could with getting his breakfast ready. I wouldn't have anything to eat. I would just leave the house without saying anything to him. I would receive phone call after phone call on my mobile as I went to work. If I ignored these calls, he would telephone my workplace as soon as I reached there. He would then demand to know why I'd ignored his phone calls and ask me why I'd been" such a bitch" to him.

"I've fucking told you I won't be ignored. Why

Sour Face

aren't you answering me? I won't have you fucking sulking like a cunt".

"I'm not sulking. I just don't want to be upset before I go into work, I'm trying to compose myself", I replied.

"What about fucking me, you selfish bitch. It doesn't matter to you that I'm upset. I have to go to fucking work too", he would shout.

I'd always find myself apologising to him. I would promise to make sure that I'd get up at a more reasonable time in the future. He would never apologise for his behaviour. He felt that neck grabbing and name-calling was not abuse. Giving a woman a "few slaps is abuse. I thought even a stupid sour face like you would know that", he would sneer.

CHAPTER FIVE

He'd been released from court for half an hour when the telephone calls began. In the first phone call he told me he was sorry for hurting me. He blamed the aggression on the alcohol. He couldn't remember hitting me. He was still drunk when he was arrested. So he said. It was my fault for answering him back. I should have kept quiet "you know I hate mouthy, disrespectful women". He asked me to "come home". I refused. I did want to go back. It was what I knew. I'd grown to accept his abuse, as part of our relationship. I felt I could make a difference. I could make him change.

It's important to bear in mind when looking at domestic violence that if the removal of abuse is reinforcing, then the more severe the abuse, the greater the reinforcement when the abuse is stopped. The victim will see the return to the pleasurable times in the relationship, as a great prize. So this cycle becomes influential in deciding the victim's behaviour in their wish for reinforcement. If the victim leaves the abuser, any feelings of shock or depression will be substituted by stress and anxiety at loosing this powerful emotional bond. The victim will link the relief of stress and anxiety with having a relationship with the abuser, due to the conditioning that has happened. This increases the probability of the victim returning to the relationship. This research has helped me to understand why I defended him, why I felt I couldn't leave even though I knew I had too for my own safety and sanity. I knew the way he treated me was wrong, but the responsibility I felt for him, meant that I didn't want to let him down.

I was a victim of traumatic bonding. I was suffering from battered woman syndrome. I can see that now. Back then I hadn't heard of these subjects. I didn't think I was a victim. Not me. No way. I thought I was in love with someone who had a few psychological problems and who needed that extra bit of support. The abuse (severe rages and outbursts of temper) was part of his problems. He couldn't help it .So I thought. But there was this tiny part of me, telling me, that even though I wanted to go back to him, I couldn't. It would be wrong and dangerous. He told me he was going to walk around the city.

"I've got on a bus and gone into town. Don't know where I'm walking. You don't know what it is like being locked in a prison cell. They treat you like an animal. It's not at all nice. You know I've been through it before. I can't believe you told them about my previous conviction. You really are a sour face bitch", He was shouting.

"They did a police check, before they asked me if you had any previous convictions. You have. I'm not lying. I'm telling the truth". I stood up to him.

"If you really loved me you would have protected me. I knew from your behaviour that you couldn't wait to get the knife in. It's true what they say about kicking a man when he is down", he said mockingly.

He quickly changed the subject.

"I'm not going back to that fucking hole of a house. It's not fucking home unless you're there. My life isn't worth living without you. I may as well be

dead. You'll be sorry then".
I was horrified "Don't say that everything will be OK", I tried to reassure him.
"No it won't be. Not if you don't come back to me", he pleaded.
"I'm not coming back to you", I replied.
"That you'll see what's going to happen. I hope you can live with yourself".
He hung up. I rang him back and reached his voice mail. I tried again and the same thing happened. I telephoned his mother, as I was worried about him. Yes I know, how ridiculous that sounds. He had beaten me up, treated me so badly, and I was still concerned about him. I was worried about how he would cope on his own. I felt responsible for him still. I have explained the reasons for my feelings. About ten minutes after I telephoned his mother. He rang me,
"You really are a mad bitch. As if I'd hurt myself over a sour face cunt like you. I'm telling you not to fucking ring my mother again. She's very upset because of what you've done, getting me arrested. There was no need to go that far," he was screaming at me, as I hung up.
He continued to ring me at ten-minute intervals. The phone calls varied. He'd be upset; crying and begging me to go back to him. In the next phone call he'd be aggressive: screaming his favourite names for me into my ear. I'd hang up. The calls continued throughout the evening at minute intervals, until he threatened to come round to Jill's house and kill me if I didn't" go back home". I reported this along with the other calls I'd received that day to the police, who visited Darren and Jill's

Sour Face

house. By the time they arrived the calls had settled down. They were now only arriving one every twenty minutes. He rang whilst the police were still present.

"It's me. There's no fucking milk in the house. I want a cup of tea and there's no fucking milk."

"I know there's no milk. You need to go to the shop and buy some", I replied. The police officers remained in the room.

"Why are you repeating what I'm saying? Who have you got there? You are a fucking bitch. I hope you're not trying to get me arrested again. I don't want to go back to that cell. I couldn't bear to be locked up like an animal again. I didn't mean I was really going to kill you. Please don't tell the police", he began to cry.

"I won't ", I replied, feeling such a hypocrite as I looked at the two policemen standing in front of me.

The tone of his voice changed becoming hard and harsh.

"I knew you wouldn't. You are as soft as belly ache shit. You've got no fucking backbone, can't stand up to anyone. I'm not going to any fucking shop for anything. I'll go without first. We both know the shopping is your fucking job". With those words he hung up.

The police felt that he just wanted to hear my voice. He would find any excuse to talk to me. They advised me to switch the phone off, and to let them know if there were any more threats in the future. I did as they advised, but felt very annoyed that I had to turn my phone off. The only means of communication I had with anyone. I felt even more isolated and alone. When I turned my phone back on the next day there were numerous missed calls all from his number.

As soon as I switched my phone on he rang. I answered. Why? I did so because I was still in my conditioned state of mind. I was really worried about him. I was worried that he hadn't gone to work, and that he might lose his job. I felt that would be my fault. I was worried about him not eating or doing any shopping, I was worried that he hadn't any clean clothes, because he didn't know how to use the washing machine. All I could think about was his needs. All I'd thought about for two years was him. His needs and wants were my life. I didn't think about myself at all. As long as he was happy then my life was ok. He asked me to go to see him in a local shopping centre. He wanted to sort out the house with me. He couldn't afford to stay there. (I will explain about my house later). I was only prepared to pay my half of the mortgage and nothing else, as I wasn't living there. He told me he couldn't afford it and that I should move back in. He would move out. He still felt that once I'd moved away from" your fucking mates influence, they've never liked me" and I was living on my own in the house we once shared, I would miss him so much, that I'd want to give our" relationship another try." I just wanted to go home. I also wanted him to see my face. I wanted him to see what he'd done to me, so I agreed to meet him.

I met him in a local shopping centre. He

continuously rang me, for half an hour before we were due to meet, asking me where I was, every few minutes. He stood in the market place surrounded by people. I walked towards him feeling a mixture of fear, anxiety and relief. Strange feelings to have but I was so relieved to see him again. Him and my life with him was my routine. It was my way of coping with the stress of the abuse as described by Walker. Then I thought I was losing the plot by wanting to see him again. He stared at my face and me.

"If that's what I've done to you then I'm a fucking monster. I don't deserve you", were his opening words.

"You know very well what you've done to me. You have seen the police photographs. The bruising has improved over the past few days", I replied.

"I know why you've come here today. You want to punish me for what I've done. I can see why you want to do that. I don't hold it against you. I forgive you".

I was angry with him.

"You forgive me. You've got a dam nerve. Have you seen what you've done to me? I think it should be the other way round mate."

"Don't shout at me bitch. You are the one who went to the police and had me arrested. You chose to do that. You wanted to punish me".

"What you did to me was wrong. Why won't you believe that? I didn't do anything to deserve this abuse. I had no choice I had to report these injuries to the police. Look at them. How would I explain the extent of these injuries to the people who care about me? They would want to know how I had injured myself ".

"I don't fucking care about what anyone else thinks. That's your fucking problem. You listen to other people too much. I bet you've been discussing our relationship with any fucker who'll listen. You are always desperate for attention miss fucking dim wit."

"I'm not staying here for you to speak to me like that again" I moved away from him.

"Don't go. I'm sorry. Look we need to sort this out. Please stay. I won't shout. I promise. Let's just sit on this bench and talk". He looked at me with tears in his eyes.

I sat on the bench, putting my handbag between us.

"Thank you for staying. Are you coming back to me?" he asked.

"No. I can't live with you any longer. I can't let you treat me the way you have been. This beating is the last straw", I replied.

"I won't ever treat you that way again. I don't blame you for not believing me. Give me another chance to prove to you that I can and will change. I've found a bed-sit. I'll move out and then you can move back into the house. It's your house anyway. I hate the fucking place. And you can give me back the watch I bought you and my phone. I want my money as well you fucking bitch. Half of that money in the savings book is legally mine. I can't believe you took the fucking savings book. You can give me back every thing I ever gave you. I don't want you keeping anything I bought for you. You fucking sour face bitch".

He moved towards me. I jumped up. I physically

flinched.
"That's it. I'm going. I'll move back in at the weekend after you've moved out. We'll sort legal matters out after that". Without looking at him, I turned and headed towards the car park.

The phone calls continued during that first week of our separation. They continued to vary in content, from him begging me to go back to him, to spiteful, threatening comments. I switched my phone off for long periods of time. He would then telephone my work place continuously until I spoke to him, demanding to know why I had my phone switched off. I didn't want him interfering with my work life. I'd worked too long and too hard to have my professional life destroyed by his erratic behaviour. In order to prevent this I would leave my mobile switched on to silent when I was at work. He was content to leave me numerous voicemail messages, so he stopped ringing the landline at work.

The situation came to ahead on the Thursday evening. My face was badly bruised, but I wasn't going to stay at Jill's house moping. One of our other friends asked us both to go to her flat for the evening, and we accepted her invitation.
He rang me, to finalise the moving out arrangements.
"I am moving out tomorrow afternoon. I'm taking all of my personal belongings. Everything that is mine is coming with me, including the television, and both the CD and DVD players. You will have to buy fucking new ones. Make sure you move

back in tomorrow night. I don't want this house being left empty. It will be a target for burglars when the neighbours see me moving all my possessions out of the house. Are you going out over the weekend?" He asked.

"It's none of your business what I do or where I go", I answered.

"That means you're going out. You fucking bitch! I can't believe you'd go out with your face such a fucking mess. Every one you meet round town will think I'm a complete bastard, that's what you want you them to think".

"That's not my problem. I can assure you that my mission in life isn't to make other people hate you. I'll do what I want when I want. You can't tell me what to do anymore, because I won't let you", I was getting angry.

"Don't fucking cross me bitch. I'm sick of telling you. I won't be screeched at by, a fucking sour face bitch. If you go out around town tonight, or any night whilst you're face is in that mess, I'll come and find you, hunt you down like a dog, and stab you dead."

"I'm not having you threatening me anymore", I was shouting at him.

"It's not a threat bitch. It's a promise. I'll stab you dead".

"That's it. I'm going to report you to the police. You can't carry on behaving like this towards me. I won't let you".

"I'll do what I fucking want. No fucker tells me what to do. Go to the fucking police. You're very good at that, fucking cunt", he was screaming at me now.

Sour Face

I hung up. My hand was shaking as I dialled the number of the local police station.

I reported the threats to the desk sergeant; he took all my details and gave me a new crime number .He informed me that police officers would come and see me over the weekend. He felt there was no immediate risk to me as there had been no further threats and he hadn't turned up at my friend's house.

The phone calls continued but I ignored them eventually turning my phone off. Jill and I drove to our friend's house where we all spent the evening together. I remained on edge for the majority of the evening.

The next day he rang me and I answered his call.

"I want my fucking money from our savings account. I fucking want it today", he screamed at me. "If you fucking turn your phone off again, I'll come to your fucking mate's place, even if her fucking stupid bloke is there, wherever you are I will find you and you'll be made to regret turning the fucking thing off".

"I don't want to meet you", I replied.

"I fucking don't care what you want bitch. I want my fucking money. I'll meet you outside the bank at three o'clock. You better make sure you're there. Alone, that means no fucking mates with you. I don't want anyone else interfering in our business. "He hung up.

The telephone rang again. I felt sick with nerves as I answered it.

"I meant what I said. I'll make you sorry if you don't come to the bank to meet me today alone.

"Stop threatening me" I answered.
"Listen miss prim fucking sour face. I'm not threatening you at all. What I'm doing is making you a promise. There is more than one way to skin a cat. There are people you care about; like your fucking kids, whose praises you always fucking sing".
"You wouldn't dare hurt them". I was panicking.
"Don't fucking dare me bitch. I can do what I want when I want and there is fuck all you can do to stop me. Three o' clock outside the bank be there", he ended the conversation.
Jill heard him shouting. "I'm not sure you should go alone", she was worried.
"I've got to go. He won't stop harassing me until he's got what he wants, and that's the money. I'll keep in touch with you by phone, any sign of aggression and I'll phone the police", I tried to reassure her. I wasn't convincing her or myself. He was still controlling me. I hadn't learnt how to say no to him. I still thought I could manage his behaviour. How wrong I was.
Whilst I was driving he rang me at two-minute intervals to find out where exactly I was.
"I'm on the way. I can't go any faster, there are road works everywhere", I told him.
"You need to hurry the fuck up. I'm fucking waiting for you bitch", he shouted.
I found myself running up the high street. He had so much control over me. He said jump and I asked how high.
 I stood outside of the bank; there was no sign of him.
My phone rang. I answered it. "I can see you

Sour Face

fucking bitch. Don't bother trying to look for me. Now go inside the bank and get my money".

Inside the bank I stood in the queue becoming extremely anxious with each minute that went past. After what appeared to be an eternity, I found myself in front of a cashiers' window. I explained that our relationship had ended and that I wanted to withdraw half of the money that was in the savings account.

They refused to give me his half of the money. The reason being there wasn't enough cash on the premises. They would have to order the money. It would be ready for collection on Monday.

I stood at the counter tears flowing down my badly bruised face.

"He won't believe me", I sobbed." He'll think I'm keeping the money from him on purpose".

The counter assistant looked at me with utter distain .She didn't see me as an equal or as a professional woman. Her interpretation of what she saw in front of her was a pathetic wreck of a person who had allowed her self to be abused by a man. This was illustrated perfectly by her following statement.

"Send him into me and I'll tell him. He can't have any money until Monday. That's the best I can do," she said in a superior manner. It's very easy to be judgemental and smug when you are sitting behind a bullet- proof screen with a panic button at your finger- tips, knowing that help will arrive in minutes if you need it.

I left the building society. He was nowhere to be

seen. After a few minutes he appeared from behind me.

"Where's my money?" He demanded.

"You can't have it until Monday. They have to order the money in. Go and ask at the counter if you don't believe me". I sounded desperate.

"I'm not fucking going in there. Not after you've just been in. They'll know that we are together and that I'm responsible for you face. They will think I'm a bastard and we both know I'm not"

He stopped talking and stared at me.

"Have you cleaned your teeth today", he asked. "They look fucking filthy .I don't know how you can walk about in public with your fucking face in that state. It's still a fucking mess".

I was amazed at the change of direction the conversation was taking.

"I haven't eaten a thing for days. I'm making myself ill. I'm wasting away. You will be fucking sorry then won't you, when I end up in hospital fucking ill because of the way you've treated me, by not forgiving me and moving back in the house ", he continued. He scanned me up and down. "I bet you're still fucking eating. You've always been a greedy cow".

I'd lost six kilograms in weight in two weeks, now weighing well under eight stone. I wasn't eating or sleeping. I looked pale, tired and drawn.

"I' m not eating much. I haven't got much of an appetite."

"You don't look like you've lost weight to me. You've still got your big stomach. You're still a fat cunt".

"Where are you going now", he asked me.

Sour Face

"To town", I answered.

"Well, I might see you there. I can go where I want, and there's nothing you can do to stop me. Call for the police. They can't do anything. You came here to meet me today .Of your own free will. No one will believe you that I'm doing anything wrong. They certainly won't believe you that I threatened you or your kids. I'll deny everything any way. Your word against mine, nothing can be proved. They'll just think you're a lying cunt", he sneered at me.

"I can wait until Monday for my money," he changed the subject again." You can give the money to my mother. She'll meet you here at twelve o'clock. Make sure you clean your teeth before you meet her". He turned away from me and headed in the direction of the multi- storey car park.

The next day, at 9am, two police officers came to my friend's house. They wanted to take a statement regarding the events of the previous Thursday evening. I explained to them he had not made any further threats to kill me and that I had seen him the previous day. They both felt that his behaviour was intimidating. As I had believed on Thursday he would be capable of coming to find me and physically hurt me, together with his previous convictions, and the fact he had beaten me seven days earlier, they felt there was enough evidence to charge him with threats to kill me. They would charge him with this offence with or without my cooperation. I decided to co operate and gave a statement regarding the events of the previous day.

I told the police that I felt very let down by the local magistrate's court, and that I'd written a letter to them disagreeing with their decision, allowing him back to the house. They took a statement from me and went to arrest him. The second time he'd been arrested in two weeks.

He appeared in court the next day. He had legal representation from the same solicitor. This time I had not bothered to contact victim support. I just couldn't see the point of having to wait for two days for the outcome of the court case. I contacted Bernie who was present in the public gallery. She was able to let me know the details of the case as soon as the hearing was over. He pleaded not guilty to threatening to kill me.

This time the magistrates were firmer with him. It was a week to the day he had appeared before them charged with assaulting me. He was given bail and a trial date set for two weeks later. He was ordered to leave the house, reporting to the police station on a daily basis until his hearing date. He was not allowed to contact me, which included coming to the house, my work place, by phoning me, sending me letters or e-mails, or via a third party. He was not allowed to enter the street where we lived. Failure to comply with any of these conditions would result in bail being broken and him being re arrested. His belongings would be collected by a police officer and taken to his new address. His solicitor also requested that I was not allowed to contact him either. If I did, this would result in the case against him being dismissed.

CHAPTER SIX

He loved to insult me before I went to work. He would always tell me my breath smelt, my teeth were dirty and that I needed to go to the dentist. Despite my big fear of dentists I found myself having regular visits to both the dentist and the hygienist. He would then constantly nag me about how I looked after my teeth.

"Look at the state of your fucking teeth. Have you cleaned them today?"

"Of course I have. I wouldn't leave the house without brushing them". I was annoyed with him.

"Well, they look fucking filthy. You haven't fucking flossed them this morning", he would stand in front of me checking my mouth, holding my chin in his hands.

The reason he gave for this behaviour was the cost of going to the dentist was so expensive and I'd be wasting money if I didn't continue to look after them.

"Do you know how much money we've spent on your fucking teeth, getting them decent? It's cost me hundreds of pounds. Then what happens? You don't carry on looking after them. That's such a waste of money. You are such a stupid sour face bitch. You're always spending money like water".

He would insist I brushed them for ten minutes in the morning and at bedtime. He seemed to know when I'd spent less than this length of time cleaning them. I also had to use mouthwash twice a day and gargle for one minute, finishing off with dental floss making sure that particular attention was paid to my front teeth. How he used to dent my confidence. Can you imagine? I was just about to spend eight hours a day in close contact with others when he told me my mouth stinks? I told him not to tell me. He would say, "I'm just being fucking honest. That's the best way to be with you. You need to know when you look a fucking mess".

I agree with honesty, of course I do. But there is being honest to a degree that is so brutal it destroys the other person. If you really care about someone you want to protect them, nurture them. We've all told white lies to people, not to make them look stupid or make fools of themselves, but to make them feel better, to reassure them. Not him. It had to be the whole in your face truth. He was only that "honest" with me. This principle was great until it came to him. If someone made a comment about his personal appearance, that he'd gained weight for example, he'd fret and look to me to reassure him over and over. He'd show me how insecure he really was about himself. Just for a little while then he'd blame me.

"Well it's your fucking fault if I have gained weight. You always give me too much food on my plate. You are always making fucking curries and unhealthy food. Don't make any more. I don't want any. We both know that you spend too much money on shopping. Cutting that rubbish out should reduce the weekly shopping bill".

He went on to tell me he was very slim until he met me. This was not the case. He would tell me that I was fat. I'm five foot tall, weigh eight stone, and wear dress size eight. He'd tell me my stomach was massive, that my breasts were far too big (all his other women had small breasts, so he said) He would complain that my legs were too thin, too old looking& too white. Everything was wrong with me. He told me that he thought he would never end up with someone like me. The woman he saw as his long- term partner would be very attractive with the perfect body. She would also be intelligent and a wonderful person. In other words she would be everything in his opinion I wasn't.

His needs were paramount. He had to have a cooked meal every night after work, regardless of what kind of day I'd had or how late I worked, a proper cooked meal, nothing snack like. He always had to have a roast dinner on a Wednesday, some type of meat with roast potatoes. Never boiled potatoes, as "they were shit" and he would refuse to eat them. This would mean on a Wednesday evening it would be nine o' clock when I eventually sat down to relax after I'd prepared, cooked the meal and cleaned the kitchen. He always had to sit in front of the television when he ate his meals, even though we had a dining table.
 He would call me "a fucking snob" if I suggested we use it. After he finished eating he would hand me the tray with the empty plate to take back in the kitchen. He wouldn't dream of doing that himself. He wouldn't do anything that was even vaguely domestic. Anything to do with the kitchen bored him. When I spent time in the kitchen, I bored him. When he came home from work to find

me preparing the evening meal, he would stand in the doorway with a sneer on his face,

" Look at you standing there with your sour face. That look would turn lemons sour. I hate coming home to that face. You never give me proper attention when I get home. You are always too busy fucking cooking. There's no need to be in there at this time. You should sit with me for an hour and then start cooking. I told you I can wait till later for my dinner."

When I answered him that starting cooking later would result in me not sitting down until later he would reply "you have an answer for everything. You fucking bore me to death". He would tell me how boring I was on a daily basis. It was strange how he never found what I cooked boring. He would sit in the sitting room watching television all evening, calling me at intervals to bring him cups of tea, then criticise me for spending most of the evening going backwards and forwards to the kitchen, and not spending enough time sitting with him.

I remember the very first Sunday lunch I cooked when we just moved in together. We'd been living together for two days. I asked him to help me wash up, as I'd done the cooking. He refused. I really thought he was joking. He sat on the sofa and looked at me in disgust.

"I told you I don't do anything domestic, it bores me and I don't want to do it. It's as simple as that. No one asked you to cook. You chose to, so it's up to you to clean up" I never asked him to help me with any thing again.

Once I tried to give him oven chips, they ended up

Sour Face

being thrown across the kitchen. He liked to throw things, usually food I'd cooked or was in the process of cooking. He'd take it from the saucepan or plates and hurl it across the worktops, hob and floor. Pasta made the worst mess. It stuck everywhere. Well I suppose that proved that I'd cooked it properly. It took forever to get the kitchen clean after he'd had a throwing episode. He would get even angrier with me, when I cleaned the mess up. I didn't know what he expected me to do. I couldn't leave food all over the kitchen. I just wasn't going to win.

The back of my house has a veranda type extension, with no heating of any description in it, making it a freezing cold place to be in the winter. The kitchen has no window and leads directly on to the extension. There is an extractor fan in the kitchen. When you cook in the kitchen it does generate steam-causing condensation. He hated the condensation. He would insist that when I cooked, particularly when I cooked Sunday lunch, I closed the dining room door, so that the condensation "doesn't make the fucking wall paper come off". The CD player and radio were kept in this room. The real reason he wanted the door closed was to prevent me from listening to any music whilst I was cooking.

I wasn't allowed to have a radio in the kitchen, because "I can't hear the fucking television when you have that fucking racket on".

The back door of the house had to be open as well as the window in the extension. Even in the winter, when it was snowing and raining he insisted that this regime was followed at all times. I would be in the kitchen shivering with cold. It didn't matter to him. He camped out in the sitting room with the central heating and the fire on, with the door shut tight. I resented him so much for that.

I told him "I'm not cooking any more Sunday dinners if it means I have to stay in that freezing kitchen".

"No one asked you to fucking cook, stupid sour face", he replied. "I can go with out food. I'm not a greedy fat fucker like you. If you want to keep this house nice and smart you have to look after it. Condensation will ruin everything, even a dim miss prim like you should know that".

I would only open the window very slightly until I heard him in the hallway. Then I would quickly run into the extension and open everything the way he wanted. When he left I would shut them again, he never found out.

His mother and auntie were coming to visit us. It was a Saturday morning. He always had bacon and fried egg in a sandwich, made of thick white bread with red sauce on a Saturday morning. He was always more difficult to deal with on a Saturday morning when he wasn't at work as he was always hung over. He was snappy and his comments were even more spiteful than usual. I couldn't stay in bed even when we'd got home late. I had to be up by nine. He would make me get up before him by constantly nagging me," come on, get up lazy bitch. Nine o'clock is enough of a lie in for anyone. You're turning into my mother she stays in bed all hours. We both know she's a lazy cunt". He'd stay in bed until he could smell the bacon, he would then appear at the

Sour Face

kitchen door so I could hand him his breakfast.

Once we'd come back from the pub starving. I'd made bacon and used the last of the eggs; we'd eaten it before we went to sleep. So when we got up there were no eggs in the house. He was not happy.

" You are a stupid sour face bitch. Why did you cook them? You know I like bacon and eggs when I get up not before I go to bed. I'll eat anything when I'm drunk, because I don't know what I'm doing, you shouldn't have fucking cooked. You really are a stupid bitch".

The abuse continued until I got up out of the bed, got dressed and went to the nearest shop to buy six eggs. I cooked them for him and handed him his sandwich and tea. He never said thank you, just took the plate and cup from me, and gave them back to me empty when he'd finished.

His agitation prior to his family's visit made me panic. I asked him to contact them to find out what time they were coming. He told me they were on their way. I wasn't dressed or showered, but he still had to have his bacon and fried egg sandwich. I was stressed out by his behaviour and told him so. He began to shout at me. "Stupid whore and sour face bitch. What's the matter with you? You should have got up earlier then you'd be ready". He took the sandwich I'd made and threw it across the kitchen I'd just finished cleaning. Fried egg yolk dripped down the tiles at the back of the hob, bread stuck to the floor, red sauce smeared across the cooker top, bits of bacon landed in the sink. I stood there and cried. At that time I just couldn't cope with him being so spiteful. He

grabbed me by the neck, screaming in my face,
"You fucking spiteful bitch. I don't fucking like you, in fact I hate you, and so does my family. They pretend to like you to please me. No one could like a fucking sour face like you. You're always a cunt whenever my family visit. That's the reason they won't visit here. It's because of you and you're behaviour".

"That's not true. They don't come to see us because you don't want them here. You don't want any one visiting"

"That's fucking right. I don't want anyone interfering in our business. We are fine on our own. I don't understand the need to keep on asking people round. You're fucking mad", he screeched at me.

The doorbell rang. He went to answer it, leaving me to clean the kitchen. I'd got the last bit of egg of the tiles by the time his mother came in. I had to apologise for not being dressed, as he'd made some sarcastic remark about me lying in bed till all hours. I made the tea, served it then went upstairs to get washed and dressed, leaving him to charm his mother and auntie in my absence.

On the only other occasion his mother visited us, she brought one of her children with her. They first went to the local fish and chip shop and brought their supper to my house to eat it.

He was angry and wound himself up when they first arrived, as they wanted cutlery, plates and glasses. I wasn't expecting them to visit so I had loaded the dishwasher, which hadn't finished its cycle. In front of them he demanded to know why I hadn't enough forks for everyone to use and why

Sour Face

hadn't I emptied the dishwasher. I had to explain that it was actually washing the dishes.

"Why haven't we got enough knives and forks? You've got millions in that drawer. Go and get them out of the dishwasher lazy bitch".

"The dishes are actually washing. The machine is full of hot water. I'll scald myself if I open it now. As soon as I can I'll empty it and make sure everyone has what they need", I answered.

He accepted this and went with his family into the dining room to eat. I left them to have their supper, there was nowhere for me to sit as all the chairs were being used, so I went into the sitting room. A few minutes later he came in.

"What are you doing in here? You are fucking showing me up again, stupid sour face bitch". He turned the television off, stood in front of me and grabbed my face with both of his hands, squeezing it tight. "Now go in there and treat my family with some fucking respect you sour face whore". He let me go. I stood there trying so hard not to cry. Tears made him worse. He felt that I cried on purpose to make him feel sorry for me. I didn't. I cried because he physically hurt me, causing me pain. He wouldn't accept that. He waited until I had composed myself, and we went into the dining room together, where I played the role of the perfect host, waiting on them, making sure they had everything they could possibly want, for the remainder of the visit. He sat with them, joking, laughing and being his usual charming self (as he was in public), like a king in his castle.

Friday was the busiest day of the week for me,

the start of my busy weekend. He didn't like me cleaning the sitting room on a Saturday when it was his day off; as he spent the entire morning sprawled on the sofa watching television, and didn't like to be disturbed.

"I've been working all week. I need time to relax. I hate you fucking cleaning on a Saturday. You should do the cleaning in the week, after you've finished work. There's nothing stopping you. You really are a lazy sour face bitch".

The fact that I'd been to work for nine or ten hours a day didn't matter. Working in the library was far more demanding than my job. According to him my job was easy, "any fucker could do it".

The afternoon was spent either visiting his family or going to look around the shops in a shopping centre of his choosing. (We would then always have sex on our return. It was what he wanted and what he expected. This was followed by a fish and chip supper, with mushy peas, two slices of white bread with full fat butter and a pot of tea. It didn't matter if I didn't want this meal; this is what he had on a Saturday and he wouldn't change this routine for anyone.) This meant that the majority of the housework had to be completed before he got home from work on a Friday evening. The house had to be cleaned from top to bottom every week.

"You have to keep this house to the high standard it's at. No good decorating or buying new furniture if you're not going to look after it", he would lecture me.

If I objected because I was tired or didn't feel like it, I would be subjected to prolonged episodes of verbal and physical abuse. It was easier to do the

Sour Face

cleaning. He would check that I had cleaned the house "properly". He would pull the sofas from against the wall to check that I'd cleaned underneath them; he would the check the corners of the room to ensure that there was no dust collected there. Even though he hated the kitchen, he would always check that it had been cleaned correctly. He would run his finger in the gap behind the taps, then along the underneath of the spout on the mixer tap. He would also check the plughole in the sink for any signs of tea stains. Likewise the cups and teaspoons were checked for the same stains daily. The sink had to be cleaned with bleach then scrubbed to a shine on a daily basis. He would pull the knob controls off the hob, to check for signs of grease, so I would take them off and scrub around them with a green scouring pad. The inside of the oven had to be cleaned every week with an appropriate oven cleaner, he would open the oven door and run his finger across the bottom of the oven floor looking for signs of grease.

The window cleaner came to the house every month to clean the outside of the windows. On the same day, I had to come home from work and clean all the inside windows. It didn't matter if I had an early start at work or a late finish, the windows had to sparkle or else paying for a window cleaner was a "waste of fucking money. May as well cancel him and you could do the outsides as well".

When the window cleaner was on holiday in the summer I was expected to stand in the blazing heat (one of those rare British summer days), and clean the patio window. He couldn't wait until the window cleaner returned from holiday."The windows are too fucking filthy to wait for him. You need to stop being so fucking lazy".

During the winter, children had thrown a snowball at the windows. He noticed a mark on the window when he came into the house after work.

"There's a great big dirty mark on the sitting room window. Didn't you see it when you came in", he demanded.

"No", I replied, "Probably from the lads who were playing outside ".

"Fucking kids shouldn't be playing outside the house. They've done it on purpose, just to wind me up. You should have gone outside and told them to clear off. That window looks a right mess. Go and clean that mark off", he walked into the kitchen.

"You're being ridiculous", I was angry with him."It's dark and freezing cold outside. How stupid would I look trying to clean the window when I can't even see where the mark is suppose to be. You are over reacting. I'll sort it out tomorrow".

"Don't tell me I'm fucking over reacting bitch, because you're too fucking lazy to do any cleaning. Leave the window then. See if I care. Three fucking grand those windows cost. You want to leave them a mess then that's up to you".

He went into the sitting room and ignored me for the rest of the evening. What a welcome break from his usual abuse that was. The next day when I checked the window the dirty mark had disappeared.

He constantly told me that the house was "filthy"

Sour Face

and that I was not a" very thorough cleaner", and that I took "too long cleaning", How I resented that. I found his criticism so very annoying. He wouldn't lift a finger to help me but would tell me that I hadn't done the cleaning properly. Yes, I did lose my temper and tell him what I thought of him, but I was made to regret it, as me answering back always-resulted in physical violence.

CHAPTER SEVEN

One Friday at the beginning of our relationship, we stayed at his auntie's house. We usually stayed there when we went to a particular club as it was within walking distance. This meant we could spend some quality time with his auntie who lived alone and who welcomed the company. Most importantly it meant" we won't have to spend over twenty pounds in fucking taxi fare to get back home" .We had been drinking all evening and into the early hours of the morning. He didn't like me drinking alcohol, and picked a fight with me inside the club, this continued outside of the building. He dragged me into an alleyway between the club and the cinema. I screamed. I didn't know what he was going to do to me. He grabbed me by the neck, as he pushed me backwards I stumbled and my foot came out of my shoe. He picked my shoe up and threw it over the wall. He held me against the wall by my neck. "Just shut up bitch. You're drunk. Look at the state of you. Get in the fucking cab and behave yourself". He let go of my neck, and then he head butted me, knocking his head against my forehead.

I began to cry. This increased his anger.

"Why do you always have to spoil our evenings by being so fucking nasty? You should leave the alcohol alone if that's what it does to you. It's obvious you can't handle drink". He spat the words in my face.

He griped my arm tightly, and dragged me out of the alley and up the street to the nearby taxi rank. I hobbled behind him, wearing just one shoe.

Sour Face

What a sight I must have looked .My eye makeup was smudged through my crying. Black marks were visible underneath both eyes. My toes were poking through holes in my tights caused by walking on the rough wet pavement without the protection of foot ware. I had to go with him I had no choice. He had the house keys, my phone and my money. All of my other belongings were in my overnight bag. This bag was at his auntie's house. He pulled me inside the cab, sitting next to me holding my forearm tightly throughout the journey. He increased the grip on my arm as we left the taxi and walked up the path leading to his auntie's house. Once inside the house, he let go of my arm. He then gripped my hair in both hands. Walking backwards he pulled me up the stairs by my hair, whispering abuse all the way up the staircase,

"You are a fucking drunken whore. I know why you were screaming in the fucking alleyway. You were trying to get me in fucking trouble, fucking sour face cunt".

I hobbled up the stairs behind him trying so hard to fall. When we reached the bedroom, he let go of my hair and closed the door. I sat up on the edge of the bed. He then slapped me across the face so hard; I fell backwards onto the bed, blood pouring from my lip.

"Look what you've done. My mouth is bleeding," I sobbed.

"Fucking shut up, fucking cunt, fucking drama queen. If you weren't such a cunt to me none of this would happen, Stop fucking crying. You'll wake up my auntie".

His auntie knocking on the bedroom door, asking if I was all right interrupted him. . He went to the door and opened it slightly, just enough to put his head out, leaving his body inside the bedroom.

"Yeah, she's fine. She's really drunk. She's got a problem with alcohol, makes her difficult to deal with. It won't happen again. We're really sorry she woke you up. Go back to bed and I'll sort her out", he spoke softly, reassuring his auntie.

He came back inside the room, stood in front of me and hit me across the left side of my head. This time I saw stars. "That's for waking my auntie up, noisy drunken bitch, now get to fucking sleep".

The next day I had a swollen lip. His auntie saw my face but never mentioned it or the events of the previous night. He made a point of telling his auntie that I had been so drunk the previous night that I had lost my shoe. "That just shows you how drunk she was. I don't know how she allows herself to get in such a state." I just sat on the sofa in silence as the conversation went on around me as if I wasn't in the room. It was pointless me saying anything in my own defence as no one would listen.

As we travelled back to our home, he nagged me constantly, throughout the journey, which took about an hour and a half.

"You fucking cunt. I can't believe you showed me up in my auntie's house. You are a fucking whore. My auntie was in a right state thanks to your behaviour. I don't know how you can forgive yourself. Is that how you get your kicks by upsetting an old lady? Don't look at me like that with your sour face. That'll look would turn lemons

Sour Face

sour. You make out you're such a miss prim, nothing could be further from the truth. You are a drunken whore. You have a massive issue with alcohol. You are just like my mother. She becomes a fucking loud mouth whore when she's been drinking. All women are the same. You are a horrible fucking bitch when you are pissed."

This nagging, went on for most of the day. He constantly repeated the same sentences and words over and over .He talked about nothing else but my unacceptable behaviour parrot fashion for the rest of the afternoon and into the early evening. By the end of the day I was completely washed out, exhausted from this constant stream of verbal abuse. I apologised for my behaviour. I telephoned his auntie to apologise for any upset I had caused her. She reassured me that I hadn't upset her. She was concerned about me, asking me several times if I was feeling all right. I told her I was fine, and she appeared settled with this answer.

From then onwards I would always watch how much alcohol I drank when we were out. He of course would drink want he wanted and behave how he wished. He would never have anything to eat prior to going out for a drink, as it would then "take longer for the alcohol to work". When he was very drunk he would talk about how much he wanted to be a "writer". How he could write amazing books, and make lots of money.

"I want to write. I could write about my life. I could tell everyone how all the women I have ever known have treated me like shit. Everyone I care about has always let me down. The book would be amazing. Every fucker would want to read it. I'd be loaded with money".

"That's a great idea. You've had a very colourful life. Start writing ideas and memories down in a little notebook." I would encourage him.

I think fair play to anyone who wants to follow his or her dreams. Also while he was rambling on about his writing, he wasn't being physically or verbally abusive towards me. He wouldn't write anything down. It was just something for him to say, to brag about, and to make him appear important, superior to me. I was far too stupid to exist, let alone string sentences together on paper.

I want to explain about the verbal abuse he used against me. There would be continuous name-calling. Not just during a heated argument. (I know we've all said things we've regretted in temper). This would be on a daily basis, numerous times a day. It got to the point where he never called me by my Christian name. He would always use one of the names he had selected for me. These were usually sour face or cunt. He would tell me I was needy and pathetic. He would tell me that I needed a man in order to function. In his opinion I couldn't cope on my own. He would stress that no other man would find me attractive because I was an ugly cunt.

Research into domestic abuse, shows that all perpetrators use very similar verbal abuse towards their victims. Names include: whore, slut, tart and cunt. They all say that the victim is useless at housekeeping, a bad mother, and a useless wife

Sour Face

or partner. They use any kind of words or name-calling that makes the victim feel bad about them selves. This includes remarks about being too fat or too old, or ugly. They call their victims stupid; tell them they are mad, and that no one likes them. I was surprised to learn this. That there is a pattern to this verbal abuse and that it wasn't just me who would be called these awful names. Other victims suffer the same abuse. That's what we have to realise it is. That it is abuse and nothing else. We need to stop making excuses for the perpetrators behaviour. He behaved aggressively towards me because he wanted to. Not because he was tired, or stressed, or not feeling very well. He like all perpetrators behaved like this because he was a bully. They make a conscience decision to behave that way towards their victim. They behave that way because they want to. They want to hurt and upset their victims.

Anyone who hasn't been a victim, will read those words and think" yes, and your point is what"?

The point is until you realise you are a victim, you can't move on or out of the situation you find yourself in.

I know I'm not stupid or dim, but I was made to believe by him that I was. I was successful in my job, well liked by my peers, but when I went home at night and put my key in the front door I became a different person. That person could not make any decisions about anything by her self, because they were unable to as they were "mentally challenged". My sense of self worth, my confidence in my appearance and my own ability was nonexistent.

"You've only got that job, because there's no one else who will do it for the pittance you get", he would scorn. "You really are a stupid bitch".

I believed him. I believed him, due to the conditioning that had taken place.

I would always look for a reason for his cruelty, examine my own behaviour, and take responsibility for upsetting or angering him.

Why would he say these things if they were not true. Why would he be physically aggressive towards me if I hadn't given him cause to do so? The thought that someone would deliberately hurt me, just because they could, never entered my head.

He didn't like the way I ate.

"You are a fucking noisy eater", he told me one day as I ate a packet of crisps.

"No I'm not", I objected.

"You fucking munch your food. I can hear your fucking jaws working and your lips smacking together, it turns my stomach".

"No one can eat crisps quietly. They're meant to make a crunching noise."

"You've got a fucking answer for every thing. Miss fucking sour face, I hate the way you fucking eat. You just don't eat like a lady. Your mouth is always open showing what food is in your gob. And you talk with food in your mouth. It's fucking disgusting".

"I only talk with my mouth full when you demand an answer from me when I'm eating", I replied.

"I can't stand that fucking noise .You are giving me

Sour Face

a head ache. Haven't you fucking finished eating them yet?"
I hadn't but threw the remaining crisps into the waste paper bin.
"It's fucking true what they say about taking the girl out of the council estate but you can't take the council estate out of the girl". He scoffed.
From that day I never ate anything that made a noise in front of him. I would stand in the kitchen to eat crisps, crackers or biscuits.
He would watch me go out of the room to eat.
"It's good to see you doing as your fucking told at last. Life is so much better when you don't wind me up. Bring me another packet of crisps before you eat yours", he called after me as I headed towards the kitchen closing the door behind me.

He would constantly tell me that I was "loud". I never thought I was. No one else has ever told me my voice was very loud. "Your voice is so fucking shrill everyone looks at you when you speak. You are always drawing attention to yourself"
Once when we were shopping I answered my phone, whilst I was talking he began scolding me;
"You're fucking shouting. Lower your voice. Everybody in the shop is looking at you. You're showing me up again".
No one was looking at me. They were looking at him shouting. I hated it when he told me I was loud, "like a fucking fish wife". I developed a habit of speaking so softly, that the person on the other end of the telephone would ask me to speak up, as they couldn't hear me.
At its best the abuse would be an hour long. At its

worst, it would go on for hours and into the night. He would always pick an argument, when there was something I really wanted to watch on television. He would wait until I was sat on the sofa, appearing relaxed and settled. Then the abuse would begin. He would stand in front of the television and nag me. He kept on going over the same points again and again. He would not stop; even when I begged him .He just would not listen. I had never come across anyone who behaved like that before. I didn't know how to deal with it. He would then turn the television off, so that all of my attention was focused on him, keeping the remote control in his hands. If I were reading he would snatch the newspaper or book out of my hand and throw them across the room. He would insist that I maintained eye contact with him at all times.

"I've told you, I won't be ignored, fucking bitch".

I would go to bed and he would follow me, continuing the verbal abuse. If I fell asleep he would wake me up to call me names or tell me how terrible I was.

"Wake up you fucking whore. You will go to sleep when I tell you can. Who do you think you are you fucking cunt. I've told you are here to do as you're told. I make the fucking rules in this house"

If I got up and came down stairs, he would follow me, grab me by the neck and push me back up the stairs. He would not stop his name calling until he was ready to do so. I would be worn out the next day. It didn't seem to affect him at all. He would never refer to the events of the previous night. His favourite names for me were: sour face,

Sour Face

bitch, Miss Prim, whore, slut, tart, cunt, stupid. He would always use the word fucking in front of each name, and shout or spit the words out at me with such distain and hatred in his voice. He gave me the impression that he hated all women; he held them in such contempt. I would never do anything to provoke this abuse. I could just walk down the stairs the wrong way and he would begin this barrage of abuse. But the thing is, at the time, while I was living this existence, I didn't realise it was abuse. I didn't like it when he called me names, but I'd make excuses for him and really believed that I deserved to be spoken to like that.
He would also like to throw things. He would toss plates across the room like a Frisbee.
 Matt and Bernie came for tea. We sat in the sitting room. He began to throw a side plate in the air, with one hand and catching it in the other hand. He dropped the plate; it landed on the wooden floor smashing into lots of pieces. He laughed as I went to get the dustpan and brush to sweep up the mess. Bernie and Matt just looked at each other. I returned the dustpan and brush to the kitchen. I sat next to him on the sofa. He picked up another plate and did exactly the same, He turned to me and whispered,
"I did it on fucking purpose. What are you going to do about it?"
 I just glared at him, and went back to the kitchen to collect the dustpan, taking the rest of the plates with me.

One particular Friday, a group of my friends were going to a seventies themed night in a local club. I asked him if I could go. He wasn't going out that night. His friends were on holiday. I asked him to come out with me, but he refused.

"I'm not going out with a group of fucking women. I'm not that fucking desperate for company".

"Shall the two of us go out then? We haven't done that for a very long time" I suggested.

"I see you every day without fucking going out with you in the evenings as well."

"Please change your mind. We have had some really fun times just the two of us", I asked him.

"There's no fucking chance of me going out with you tonight. I want to stay here on my own. I've got me. I don't need any fucker else".

He was sulking, because his friends weren't about.

"You can go where you like, it doesn't bother me".

So I telephoned my friend and arranged to meet her and our other friends in a bar in town. I made sure I was dressed appropriately. I wore a long black jumper, which covered all the top half of my body, no cleavage at all showing, thick black tights, knee length black and white checked skirt and flat boots. I didn't want to give him an excuse to prevent me leaving the house. If he thought I" looked like a whore" he would have physically stopped me from leaving .I kissed him goodnight and went out to meet my friends. We had a great time. I texted him several times whilst we were out, asking him if he was OK. I didn't receive any reply. We were drinking in the pub, prior to going into the club. Once in the club, I drank diet coke. I couldn't go back to the house in any kind of drunken state. If he thought I was the slightest bit

Sour Face

drunk, I would be in serious trouble. When I got back to the house he was still awake, sitting downstairs, in the dark watching television. I came into the room and said hello. I tried so hard not to smile or appear in the slightest that I'd had a good time or that I'd been drinking. He looked at me.

"Where have you fucking been until this time? It's one o clock in the morning". He glared at me.

"You know where I've been. I went to the seventies night with my friends. I asked you if it was alright for me to go, and you said it was", I replied.

"No I fucking never, lying bitch", he shouted.

He stood up, grabbed my neck and dragged me into the corner of the sitting room, continuously shouting abuse at me.

" Only whores and fucking tarts stay out until this time in the fucking morning".

He let me go and I went into the bathroom, trying so hard not to cry. I took deep breaths, trying to calm myself down. He followed me into the bathroom.

"Look at you; you're dressed like a fucking tart. You look like a whore. You're pathetic, a woman of your age still going to places like that club. There's only one reason that women go to places like that, and that's to get a man. All you want is some man's cock up your cunt. You're fucking disgusting".

I tried to reason with him. Deny his allegations, which of course were completely untrue .He had reached the stage of anger where I couldn't diffuse the situation. I knew he was going to be physically aggressive towards me. He slapped me across the face so hard, that he knocked me backwards and I fell into the bath. Completely in, over the side, so I ended up lying fully in the bathtub. I knocked my head as I landed against the bathroom wall. My lip was cut and bleeding badly He stood there for a few seconds, looking at me in the bath, then turned and left the room. I climbed out of the bath. I was now crying. I couldn't help it. I felt physically sick and so alone

"Where are you stupid bitch?" he shouted. "Don't get fucking staying in the bathroom all night, sulking like a fucking sour face cunt. Get back in here now", he demanded.

After this and indeed after every abusive incident, he'd act as if nothing violent had happened. And I was supposed to go along with this way of thinking. If I showed any kind of emotion towards him, anger, resentment or, pain that would mean that I was sulking, and he wasn't going to put up with that. I would have to go into the room where he was and sit next to him. If I went into another room, for some time out, or to compose my thoughts, he would follow me into that room and physically make me go into the room where he wanted to be. He would talk to me as if nothing had happened and I had to speak the same way back. Can you imagine how difficult that was? Someone has hurt you physically, called you the most horrendous degrading names, and you have to appear to be treating them "normally". Inside I was resentful and very angry, but these emotions were suppressed. Why did I let him treat me that way? I put up with it because I was conditioned. I truly believed that I could help him. The caring

Sour Face

person in me wanted to help him. I really believed that he could change, with the right support and encouragement. I didn't want to fail at this "relationship". I'd failed before. I thought I could make this relationship work, all it needed was that extra bit of effort from me, and he would stop the aggression. Of course he didn't.

"Where are your fucking keys and phone? You haven't been phoning anyone whilst you've been in that bathroom have you?" he asked me.

"Of course I haven't", I replied.

"Good for you" was his sarcastic reply.

After any aggressive attack he would always demand that I hand over my mobile phone and house keys. He would lock the front and back doors, remove the keys and take the house phone (which was portable) off its stand. He would hide these items until the next day. He did this so I was kept prisoner in the house, and couldn't call anyone for help, or report him to the police. He would follow me all around the house. He was always one step behind me. If I went to the loo he would stand in the doorway until I'd finished. I always had to have the door open, so he watched me using the toilet. He wouldn't let me have any privacy. "Real couples do everything together. That includes watching you have a piss or a shit. It doesn't bother me if you watch me. But no you won't do that will you. Too much miss fucking prim sour face snobby bitch to do anything like that. I'll do what I want in my own house. I won't have you keeping anything from me. You are a just a girl from a fucking council estate, what do you want privacy for?"

Towards the end of our relationship he stopped saying he was sorry for any physical attack. It was always my fault. If I had done as I was told, for example not gone to the nightclub, he wouldn't have been aggressive towards me. He would then tell me to go to bed, He would follow me, watch me get into bed, and then get into bed his self. His final words to me would be

" Get to fucking sleep. I can't bear to look at you. I can't believe how you've upset me. Fucking bitch"

He would then turn the light off, roll over and within a few minutes would be fast asleep, leaving me, silently crying in the dark.

It's important to understand the cycle of domestic abuse. Walker (1979) calls this cycle of abuse "the battering cycle". It's made up of three stages: a tension building stage, a period of acute violence and a stage of reconciliation. I knew by the look on his face that he was going to be violent to me. Nothing I could do would change that.

Once he'd decided to be violent towards me, once that cycle had started, it wouldn't end until he'd been violent. When he was being violent I wouldn't answer him or hit him back as I felt this would give him an excuse to hit me back even harder.

I have researched the following document written for probation officers. (Domestic Violence, a practitioner's portfolio 1999) This document states the following. It doesn't matter what the victim does during an attack. "The perpetrator will continue to be violent until the tension is reduced". As the trauma of the episode lifts the victim is

Sour Face

convinced by the abuser to stay in the relationship with apologies and promises to change their behaviour, so the cycle begins again.

CHAPTER EIGHT

As soon as we moved in together the financial control began. I was adamant that I didn't want a joint bank account. I had bad personal experiences of these accounts during my previous relationship. The thought of this happening filled me with dread. I was financially independent when I met him. Ok, I wasn't rich, by any means, but I had enough money for what I wanted, I was proud of myself that I wasn't in any debt, and my bank account was always in the black. I had told him about being financially controlled in my previous relationship. The first thing he wanted us to do was to set up a joint account. The alarm bells in my "knower" began to ring at a hundred decibel's. He began to nag me, when I tried to explain to him the reasons why I didn't want a joint account.

"I just can't do this joint account, not yet. You know I got ripped off the last time I had one. I wasn't even allowed a bankcard. I just can't risk that happening to me again", I was very anxious.

"You can't judge me for something that's happened to you in the past. I'm not like that other man you were involved with. The trouble is you don't trust me. I can't be in a relationship where there is no trust. We may as well split up now. I thought you loved me. I love and trust you. You could take all my money out of the account and leave me with nothing".

"I wouldn't do that to you. I have my own money", I was horrified he would suggest I was capable of doing such a thing.

"I only have your word for that. I have to trust you

Sour Face

but you chose not to trust me", he sounded hurt.

By me not wanting this joint account, it meant to him, that I didn't trust him. That was probably true. I didn't trust anyone where my money was concerned. I'd been so badly treated in the past.

"Let's have our wages paid into our own individual accounts and set up a joint account for the house hold bills", I suggested. "We'll both put money into this household account and all of the direct debits can be paid out of it. I'll put more money into the account than you as I earn more". It seemed like the perfect solution to me.

"No fucking chance. It's either all or nothing. You're either with me or against me. I can't fucking believe that you're behaving this way. You're acting like I'm a real bastard. You're showing me that you don't fucking trust me. You have really hurt me you bitch". He began to cry.

I found myself apologising for hurting him

He continually nagged and persuaded me about this issue until I gave in. By this point I doubted myself. He had convinced me that I was completely wrong for holding those views about joint accounts. He wanted me to close my own account. I didn't. That little part of me, which I keep talking about, "my knower", wouldn't allow me to. I kept it open for two years with just two pounds in it. When we did split up, I was so fortunate to have a single account that I could begin to use again. Without it I would have experienced severe difficulties.

I remember buying a patchwork-quilted bedspread for the house we were about to move into. I spent thirty pounds out of my own account.

He stood in the middle of the shopping centre and began to shout at me.

"You've spent thirty pounds on a sheet for the fucking bed! How fucking stupid are you".

"It's my money and I'll spend it how I want to. Your behaviour is the reason why I don't want a joint account with you", I replied.

We drove to his mother's house. All the way there, he constantly nagged me about how much money I had spent.

"You are just like a fucking child. You don't know the value of money. Money just burns a fucking hole in your pocket. You just have to spend it on anything".

I ignored him.

When we reached his mother's house, he couldn't wait to tell her how stupid I had been.

"Do you know how much money the silly cow has spent on a fucking sheet for the fucking bed?" he exploded.

"Thirty fucking pounds, that's how much she spent. Show my mother what you've been spending your money on. Don't look at me like that that. Show her", he demanded.

I pulled the bedspread out of the carrier bag.

When she saw it, she told him what a bargain I'd had. "It's very beautiful and classy. Just like the ones you see in the magazines. They cost a lot more than thirty pounds", she told him.

He then changed his tune and calmed down. He told me afterwards that he was sorry if he upset me, but he was only joking and I'd taken everything too personally. This was not true. He wasn't joking, he didn't know how.

Sour Face

We'd had the joint account for a month. We were living together at this point. It was payday. I'd recently lost a lot of weight; consequently, my jeans were now massive on me. So on the way home from work, I went into a local high street store and brought some new jeans and a t-shirt top. In total I spent forty pounds. He rang me to tell me he had left work. I told him I'd been shopping. He began to shout at me.
"You should have asked me, if it was ok to spend that money. That account has my name on it as well. It's not just your money now. It's ours"
 I answered him back, "Fourteen hundred pounds has just gone into the account. You get paid next week, another eleven hundred pounds. What is the problem?" I asked him.
"You have to realise you can't spend and save it. We both have to ask each other if we want to spend any money on anything, repeating myself, it's not just your money it's ours," was his reply.
 I found myself apologising for spending my wages without asking him first
"That's ok. Remember to discuss anything that needs to be spent with me, and everything will be fine. You just have to get used to the situation".
 This set the pattern for our financial life. If I drew any money out of the cash machine I had to tell him what I was using it for. In the end it was easier not to bother taking money out. When we went out on a Friday he would take one hundred pounds out of the cash machine. He would give me thirty pounds and keep the rest. This money he gave me would be for my night out and taxi fare home. Any change I would be expected to keep for

bread, milk or other grocery items that we needed during the week. So in effect from a salary of four hundred and fifty pounds, a week, I was given fifteen pounds to spend. If I didn't go out I wouldn't get any money .He would buy my toiletries from the budget supermarkets in his lunch hour. I would give him a list of what I needed and he would fetch them.

We shopped every two weeks on the Internet. He liked to know exactly how much the food bill came to. He would then nag me, telling me I was a bad housekeeper/ shopper if I spent" too much". He never told me what "too much" meant. No sum of money was ever mentioned. Even though I asked him on many occasions how much money was allocated to the food budget. He would complain bitterly if there wasn't breakfast, lunch, dinner and snacks in the house at all times. He would take the receipt and check every item, including the cost every fortnight. He would leave me to put the shopping away, once he'd moaned about how much money I'd spent.

I went to the supermarket to buy ingredients to make Bernie's twenty-first birthday cake. I couldn't get these items on the Internet, so it meant that I'd spent ten pounds extra that fortnight on shopping. He was sitting at the computer and I was ironing in the bedroom. He was eating a tube of crisps. I told him I'd been shopping and how much I'd spent.

"You spent how much? You are a stupid fucking bitch. I'm not made of money, you just spend it like fucking water", he yelled at me. He took the tube of crisps and threw them at me. They flew through the air and landed in various places across the

Sour Face

room.

"Look at your sour face. You are such a fucking sour face bitch. You are always standing around with that fucking sour face. I don't fucking like you. Always answering back and not doing what you're told"

He grabbed the iron that was resting on the ironing board. I thought he was going to burn me with it. I jumped out of his way. He tipped the ironing board over towards me, just catching my leg as I moved out of the way, and threw the iron, which landed metal side down on the carpet. The carpet was burnt, with an iron shape clearly visible.

"Now look what you've done, you stupid, sour face bitch. Clean that mark off, stupid sour face."

"It won't come off as the fibres have been burnt". I tried to tell him.

"When will you learn to stop fucking arguing with me and just do as you're told. I'm sick of you being so fucking lazy", he shouted.

He wouldn't listen to me. He stood there while I scrubbed the carpet with various cloths and scourers. After about ten minutes he just left me and went down stairs. The burn mark remained on the carpet.

He didn't like me giving my children any money (they were both students), unless it was for birthday or Christmas presents. At Christmas he would tell me how much I should spend on them in gifts. He always insisted that I spent the same amount on my children that he spent on his siblings, between ten and twenty pounds. I wanted to spend more money on Matt and Bernie. They were my children not my siblings. I would try to save money from reclaimed travel expenses or use my credit card to get extras for them. Items he didn't know about. I'd wrap them up and hide them in the spare room, so he couldn't find out how much I'd really spent.

Unfortunately one of my elderly relatives died. We were very close I had looked after them while they were ill. They remembered me in their will leaving me thirty thousand pounds. That money went into our joint savings account (yes, by now, we had two joint accounts), in two transactions. We went to choose furniture for the house. I knew what I wanted: a black leather sofa. I found what I was looking for in a local branch of a high street furniture store. The cost was eleven hundred pounds. He stood in the shop and said" Is that the one you want?" Yes, I replied. He turned to me, in front of the shop assistant, "OK, then, you can have it if you want". I turned to him and laughed. I thought he was joking. It was my money and I was going to buy the sofa I wanted. It was as simple as that. "Thanks", I replied looking at him. He was being deadly serious. He meant and truly believed he was giving me the sofa, or rather doing me the great honour of allowing me to buy my own sofa out of my own money.
When we first met he wanted us to go away on holiday, as he'd never been away with any of his previous girlfriends. He suggested we went to Kenya, as he had always wanted to go on a safari.

Sour Face

I thought it was a good idea. I'd never travelled any further than Europe; this would be a great adventure. He chose the resort, the hotels and what time of year we travelled.

We went to several travel agents until he found a travel agent that could give him the deal he thought we deserved. We sat in the travel agents. He turned to me.

"How are you going to pay for this holiday?" he asked.

"I'll save as usual", I replied.

"Why don't we put this holiday on your credit card? We've got a joint account now. Both of us are contributing, so we will both be paying for it".

I looked startled. It felt so wrong. I hate debt.

"Don't be a cunt about it. It's what other couples do all the time".

The travel assistant came back to us. She turned to us and asked how we were going to pay for our holiday.

"By credit card ", he replied.

I found myself taking the credit card out of my purse and handed it to the travel assistant.

 (Later that year we went to his friend's wedding. We stayed in a hotel. Again this was charged to my credit card, even though we had three thousand pounds in the joint savings account). When we split up he left me with the whole of this debt, legally it was my debt, as the card was is my name only.

As I've previously said, his catch phrase regarding money was, "you can't spend it and save it ". Every spare penny had to go into the savings account. We weren't saving for anything special;

he just wanted as much money as possible in there. Looking back on this now, my thoughts are that he knew we would eventually split up. Everyone has a breaking point. Even I wouldn't be able to accept his behaviour forever.

He once told me "I don't know how the fuck you put with me. I treat you like shit and you still stay with me".

I replied, "That's because I care about you".

"You must do either that or you're a fucking stupid cunt", he answered.

Any money in that account, legally he was entitled to half of. This would be his fund to start again.

He decided when we needed new clothes. He'd wake up on a Saturday and say "we're going shopping for clothes today". This would happen twice a year. He would decide what shops we were going to and how much we would each be spending. He would always spend more on himself than he'd budgeted for. I would be expected to spend less than he had allowed.

We went into a national supermarket chain that also sells clothing and household goods. He found a pair of shoes for me that cost four pounds. They were made of plastic. I did try them on and couldn't walk in them, they were such a bad fit that every time I tried to walk in them, my toes would scrap across the top of the shoe, my foot would come out and I would leave the shoe behind on the carpet in the shop.

"They will do for work. I've brought two shirts and a pack of ties. There's nothing wrong with the goods from here. There is nothing wrong with

Sour Face

those shoes. Look at the way you're staring at them with your fucking sour face. You are such a fucking snob".

So we brought them. I was unable to wear them as they ripped my feet to pieces, causing them to blister and bleed. I threw them away, only after we had split up. I wasn't allowed to do so whilst we were together, as that would have been a waste of money.

I remember once, buying two skirts, from a high street store. He checked how much I'd spent. I told him I'd spent the same amount as him. "That is so fucking typical of you. You've always got to have the same amount of money as me. God forbid you have any less". He then went and brought another pair of shoes from the same shop, just to spend more money than me. He thought he deserved more than me, because he was special. I wasn't anywhere as special as he was.

I was ashamed sometimes of the way I looked, at work, particularly when I went to visit other units or attend meetings. I'd turn up in my five pound blouses and skirts from a high street store that specialises in cheap clothing. The skirts would be shiny from all the washing and ironing they received. They weren't meant to last for years and years. I had the same pair of work shoes for three years. I threw them away when we split up. He said they were very ugly shoes. They probably were, but when I wanted new ones, he told me they were wonderful. They cost twelve pounds from a local cheap shoe shop. I was so ashamed of them. When the zip on my winter boots broke, I had nothing else to put on my feet but those shoes.

He became verbally abusive, "stupid bitch. What do you mean you haven't got any shoes? There's a box full in the cupboard".

When I showed him that the box actually only contained his shoes, he became even more abusive.

"You can't make me responsible for you not having any shoes to wear. I won't let you do that to me. You are a grown woman and need to take responsibility for yourself".

I did point out to him that I wasn't allowed to buy shoes or in fact anything without his permission. He just dismissed these facts and told me to "get a new pair of fucking boots tomorrow". I did. I took them home and he hated them, because he hadn't chosen them for me. He told me I looked stupid in them and that I was not to wear them when we went out together.

He brought me a designer pair of shoes with very high heels for Christmas, the last Christmas present he brought for me out of our joint account. He chose the most expensive pair of shoes in the shop; he couldn't wait to tell me how much he'd spent.

They were ridiculously high; I could only walk very short distances in them.

"I told the girl in the shop I wanted a really sexy pair of heels. She got these out for me. She really liked them and told me how lucky you were having someone like me buying them as a present for you. I could tell she really fancied me", he boasted.

Sour Face

"She's got to be nice to you. She wants to make a sale," I was now used to his comments on what a woman magnet he was.

"Sour face bitch .You need to stop being so jealous. You've got a decent pair of shoes now. There's no need to wear those horrible ugly flat shoes that you insist on wearing. You are so fucking short you need the extra height any heels can give you", he snapped.

When we split up he wanted the shoes back. I packed them with his belongings and returned them to him.

He wanted to create the perfect woman. He tried to do that with me, to turn me into his ideal woman. He would buy clothes for me and expect me to wear them if I liked them or not. He preferred me to wear skirts rather than trousers for work.

"Nothing looks smarter than a blouse and skirt." He thought I looked very womanly when I dressed in this way. "Trousers make you look like a man". He would tell me. So I stopped wearing trousers and wore skirts to work. It was easier to do what he wanted. He wouldn't insult my clothing if he had chosen it.

He wanted me to dye my hair "white blond", like Marilyn Monroe blond. It was not what I wanted. I prefer my hair to look more natural, but he persuaded me to have it dyed this white blond and to change the style. I hated it. On a trip to my hairdresser's, she advised me that my hair was now in such poor condition I needed to change the colour, and think about having a "good hair cut", to remove most of the damaged hair. I jumped at the chance to have a new hairstyle. I was nervous about going home with my new style because I knew he wouldn't be happy with me, as I'd made a decision about my appearance without consulting him. He hated my hair.

He insulted it and me for about a week then suddenly one day said to me" I prefer your hair like that. Make sure you keep that style".

His perfect woman only wore white lace under ware, sometimes pink, but never black, Black was "fucking horrible. Only tarts wear black knickers", he would tell me.

This woman would be professional, have a successful career, and be in a very well paid job. She would be softly spoken, articulate, and intelligent. Her appearance would be smart. She would wear knee length skirts, tailored blouses that never showed any cleavage, and smart sweaters. She had perfect skin, sparkling white teeth and a perfect figure. She would be a good cook, excellent housekeeper and an extremely proficient cleaner. She would never get tired or ill. He wouldn't have to do a thing in the house because she would do everything for him, willingly. She would never answer him back, accepting that she was always wrong in every argument they may have. He would be able to go out where he wanted and with whom he wanted at any time. She would not go anywhere, preferring to stay at home and wait for him. She never complained about anything. She would behave this way because she truly loved him. These standards he set were unattainable .No human

Sour Face

being could ever achieve them. When I failed to reach these high unrealistic standards, failed to become his idea of the perfect woman, I gave him the excuse he needed to punish me.

My inheritance settlement was finalised on the 2nd April. By the 2nd of July in the same year we had brought and moved into a house. He was desperate to get on the property ladder. He couldn't afford a house or flat on his own and had never owned a property. He was determined to buy a house. He behaved like a man possessed, hunting through property lists and estate agent web sites .We had six months left of the lease on our rented accommodation. There was no urgency to move. He didn't want to wait. He wanted a house and that was it. I had my money now; we could, should I say he could afford one. He argued with vendors, estate agents, everyone he came into contact with regarding the purchase of the house. Finally it was left with me to liaise with all interested parties, as they refused to deal with him.

We finally made it to the solicitor's office to sign the purchase documents. £20,000 deposit was paid. All of this money was taken from the money left to me by my relative. The house was purchased in joint names. He didn't contribute a penny towards the deposit or legal fees. The alarm bell was ringing in my knower as I signed the legal papers. I knew that owing this property with him was a massive mistake. I couldn't stop the process. By this point in our relationship I was completely in his control. When the documents were signed he looked at me with a strange smirk on his face.

"That's it I'm on the property ladder", he boasted.

As soon as we moved into the house his behaviour changed towards me. The violence, aggression and verbal abuse increased. All now happened on a daily basis.

How could I live the rest of life being physically abused? As I age my bones will become brittle. I could be hurt much more easily. My bones could be fractured. I knew I couldn't live my life the way I was living it, long term. I didn't want to grow old on my own, but I wanted to live my life feeling happy and contented. My personal view is that you don't have to be in a relationship to be happy. Those of us who choose to be need to feel comfort, respect, friendship and love from the person we are with.

If we are not treated this way then we have to leave the relationship.

I know for anyone who's in a controlled relationship, to anyone who is a victim, it's easier said than done. It's easy for anyone to say leave him, when they are not in this all consuming relationship.

No one will understand him like you can.

Who'd look after him if you weren't there?

People wouldn't like him when they find out how he's been treating you.

He'd be alone.

The people who care about you could even hurt him physically.

You'd be responsible for all that. It would be your fault.

Sour Face

You wouldn't be able to function without him.
You are useless, stupid, dim, old, and ugly. No one else could possibly want to be with you or find you attractive.
No one would ever love you like he can.
It's not like he's abusive all the time, it's only when he's tired, or had a drink, or when he's had a bad day at work. You do get a break. So you can cope.
Anyone who identifies with anything they have just read has been or is a victim of domestic abuse.
I was a victim. One thing I know now with all of my heart, none of what happened to me, or indeed to any victim, was our fault. It is the abuser's fault. They choose to behave that way.
Each time he was aggressive he would yell at me; "If you don't like it you can fuck off. You know where the door is. I'm not leaving my fucking house. I did that before when I left my wife, walked out with nothing. I'm not doing that again"
I believe that he increased his aggression towards me in order to make my life so unbearable that I would leave the property I had just purchased. He made it very clear to me that "If you fucking leave this house, don't think that you'll ever get back in, or get any of the items we've just bought. I'll make sure of that".
Why should I leave a house I had paid the deposit for and without my wages we wouldn't have been able to afford? It just wasn't fair. He didn't want the house. He wanted the money it would generate.
In the end I had to leave it. I know if I had stayed when he beat me, I wouldn't be alive today.

CHAPTER NINE

I was nervous as I dialled my line managers mobile. My voice trembled with emotion as I explained the reason why I would not be going into work that morning. That was so difficult having to tell him personal information about my life and how someone who I cared about had physically assaulted me. I felt so ashamed. I thought my boss would judge me and deem me useless at my job because I had allowed myself to be treated in this way.

To say my boss was supportive would be an understatement. His kindness reduced me to tears. I promised to stay in touch with him telling him I would return to work as soon as I had sorted out the joint account.

My face was now a mixture of black and different shades of purples. My eye remained swollen but I could open it freely. There was no natural skin tone visible at all, on the right side of my face. I did think of covering my face with foundation but it would have made no difference. The bruising was too extensive and dense to hide.

I caused quite a scene when I went out during the first week. I didn't want to go out, but I had to go to the shops for various items. The whole experience was surreal. I felt like I was in a dream. People in the street stared at my face as they walked past me. A small child in the newsagents asked their mother in a very loud voice, "Mummy what has that lady done to her face"?

The child's mother tried to hush the child and shot me a look of apology. I felt upset and so ashamed.

Sour Face

I hated the way people were looking at me. I tried to smile at the child and their mother, reassuring them that I wasn't offended. After all, the child was only voicing what everyone else was thinking.

The hardest thing I've ever done in my life was returning to work with my facial injuries so evident.
Why did I go back?
Was I looking for sympathy?
Did I want people to feel sorry for me?
Was I trying to make people blame him?
Was I just being a bitch towards him?
My answer to these questions would be another question; what was the alternative staying at my friends house moping?
I'd lost my relationship, the person I cared about and my home. The only thing I had left was my job. I couldn't afford to and certainly didn't want to lose that as well. I needed the routine of getting up in the morning, going to work, and returning tired from a full days duties. I needed something to focus on, that I could throw all of my reduced energy into. I needed a distraction from my thoughts and fears.

I rang my boss asking for his permission to return to work, as my facial injuries were extremely evident.
Again, both he and his line manager were so supportive and encouraging. Their opinion was as long as I felt ready, it didn't matter what my face looked like, and they would be more than happy for me to return to work.
I felt physically sick as I walked across the car

park into the main building. Feelings of shame, guilt and responsibility filled my thoughts. I was convinced that everyone I came into contact with would judge me weak and feeble for tolerating his abuse.

The first person I saw was a friend of mine. She came towards me, hugged me tight, told me how she'd missed me and gave me words of encouragement and support.

I began to cry, in the middle of reception.

I thought, "Oh no! If this is going to happen every time someone speaks to you are not going to be able to cope."

But I knew I had to cope. I had to work; I had bills and a mortgage to pay. No one was going to help me financially. I was on my own. That inner part of me my "knower" told me I had to cope. I went into my office and eventually composed myself. I began to open my mail and spent the majority of the day hiding in my office, keeping myself busy. I was exhausted, as I wasn't sleeping. I found it very difficult to concentrate.

A few of my friends came to see me at lunchtime. One of my friends arrived clutching a big bouquet of brightly coloured flowers with a lovely card in one hand, (that made me cry), and a crazy bright balloon in the other, (This made me laugh for the first time in a long while).

Work colleagues reaction to my injuries and me varied. Some of them just stared at the actual injuries whilst talking to me; others just ignored them completely, looking anywhere in the room rather than at my face. I found myself feeling sorry for them and would try to ease their

Sour Face

embarrassment by trying to crack feeble jokes about my appearance and how I was after the role of sue the panda in the sooty and sweep children's show.

Each time I told someone about the attack; it got easier to tell the next person. After a week I found that I could answer people's questions without breaking down in tears.

A male colleague called over to me as I walked down the corridor "God, mate what have you been up to? Who's been thumping you? They have given you the best shiner I've ever seen. Hope you got a lucky punch back at them!"

The look on my crumpled face, as I fought back the tears, to tell him what had happened to me, filled him with remorse.

"I'm really sorry mate. I was joking. I thought you had been in a car accident. I never for one moment thought that you could have been hit by your partner".

He like most of my friends and colleagues hadn't knowingly come into contact with a victim of domestic abuse. The thought that it could happen to someone they knew, very well was a shock. They thought that domestic abuse only happened outside of their professional circle. They had also believed the stereotype of a victim as portrayed in the press and media. I just didn't fit that picture.

What surprised me was that during that first week back at work several women came, at different times to my office to chat to me. They all had experienced domestic violence of different degrees and at different stages in their relationships. Some of these people I had worked with for years, and they had never mentioned the abuse before. All of them had not reported their partner to the police and had remained in the relationship. Each tale was different, but the feelings of guilt, shame and responsibility they felt for the abuse was identical.

Each one was full of praise for me. They told me that they wished they could have been like me, courageous, brave, and so strong for not hiding away and being truthful to anyone who asked me what had happened to my face.

I didn't feel any of those things they thought I was. Inside I felt like jelly. I felt so insecure, afraid, trying not to cry every few minutes, very anxious and so alone. I just wanted to be normal. I wanted my life back. I could cope with what I knew. I wanted my life to return to be as it was because deep down I missed him.

This is a classic example of the effects of traumatic bonding.

The trial was booked for the local magistrates' court. No jury would be present; the magistrates would decide the verdict. I was to give evidence against him. Due to his hostile aggressive behaviour the court decided that I was a vulnerable witness. This meant that I could give evidence via a video link in a different part of the building to him.

The day of the trial arrived. I have never felt so sick, worried and nervous in my life. I had never been in a court before my involvement with him. On entering the court I was met by a wonderful older lady, who was part of the court team that supported witnesses. She would be supporting and helping me during my time in the court. She explained that all of the support team were volunteers; many of them had also at some point in their lives been victims of crime. She herself had been a victim of domestic violence many years ago.

She led me to an area in the basement of the court. This area was set out like a sitting room with tea and coffee making facilities, a television and comfortable chairs. A section of children's toys lay in the corner of the room. Opposite was the room I would be giving evidence in. It was a small office type room, complete with two chairs, and a desk. On the desk were a television monitor and a small microphone. She explained to me the procedure for giving evidence would be exactly the same as if I was in the courtroom. The only major difference is that I wouldn't be able to see him. He would be able to see me.

The CPS representative arrived to see me. She was a pleasant professional woman in her late twenties. She informed me that he was in the court building and his solicitor had asked to meet with her. She informed me that because I had been to see him on the Friday after he had made the threats; his solicitor would argue that I was encouraging the communication from him. His solicitor was going to inform the magistrates that I was leading him on, confusing him.

"I have been controlled for two years by this man. I was traumatised by the whole break up. I'd still got the bruises; I was confused, I couldn't think straight. He kept on making all those phone calls, constantly ringing me. He'd threatened to hurt my children. I had been so conditioned to obey him. What could I do? I felt I had no choice but to go and see him. I believed that if I gave him what he wanted he would leave me alone", I was beginning to get upset.

"Well the fact that you're here and willing to give evidence against him is a big plus factor. He is aware of that". She encouraged me with a smile.

As evidence of the constant pressure I had been under from him, I produced his last mobile telephone bill. It showed he had made over four hundred-phone calls to my mobile and work telephones in five days. This piece of evidence was dismissed as not relevant by his solicitor. He was focusing on the fact that I had been to see him on the Friday, outside the bank, after he'd threatened me. He was going to try and prove that this meant I had not taken his threats seriously. It was exactly like he told me it would be. No one would believe me.

"What his solicitor has suggested is a bind over order", the CPS officer continued." That would mean that he has to keep the peace towards you for twelve months. If he breaks it by harassing you in any way, you can contact the police. He'll be arrested, be back in front of the magistrates and may go to prison. If you agree to this, you won't have to go through the procedure of giving evidence. If you don't want to accept this we can proceed, but there is no guarantee that he'll be convicted, because you went to see him after he'd made the threats. If the magistrates feel he didn't threaten you, he'll be free to do whatever he

Sour Face

wants. If you accept this offer then you will have some protection from the courts in case he does continue to harass you".

"All I want is for him to stop hounding me. I just want to get on with my life", I replied.

"Well, he says that he knows the relationship is over. He's accepted that. He's got a new job, and a new place to live. He also wants to move on. He does sound genuine". The CPS officer looked at me.

"That's all I want. I'll agree to this bind over if it stops him bothering me", I suddenly felt exhausted by the entire situation. I wanted it to be all over. I wanted to be out of that court.

The CPS officer went to inform him and his solicitor the outcome of our conversation.

Ten minutes later I was called into the court to be told by the magistrates what the outcome of the verdict actually meant to me. My supporter escorted me into the court. He had already left the court building.

The chairman of the magistrates explained to me that he had to keep the peace towards me for a year. Any harassment during that time would result in him being punished by the court. He wished me well for the future. I thanked him and my supporter and left the court building, still keeping look out for any signs of him.

When I moved back into my house, Bernie came with me. The sitting room stank. He'd been sleeping in there, rather than going to bed. The quilt and pillow from our bed had been thrown on the floor. Screwed up in the corner of that room was a letter addressed to me from the police. He had opened it and obviously read it. The letter stated that I had been assessed as being a high-risk victim of domestic violence. There were various leaflets enclosed in with the letter giving information about the various local support groups for victims of domestic violence. He had ripped these up. They lay in pieces on the sofa. The windows were closed and locked. The back door was locked and bolted. It took me a while to find the back door key. He'd taken it from its usual place and hidden it in the kitchen drawer. There were items of his clothing scattered on the floors in several rooms. The kitchen worktops were full of junk food packages: fish and chip wrappers, burger boxes, numerous family size pizza boxes and take away curry trays. The waste paper bin in the sitting room was full to the brim with chocolate bar and crisp wrappers. I was amazed by the amount of food one person had eaten in six days. Bernie helped me clear up the mess. We then packed all of his belongings into suitcases and placed them in the hall ready for the police to collect. I washed and dried all of the dirty clothing he had left around the house, much to Bernie's disgust. I couldn't help it. I still felt that it was my duty to look after him.

His belongings remained in the hall for three days. No one came to collect them. I was very concerned. I knew he needed all of his clothes for work. I rang the police station to find out what was happening. They informed me that he needed to contact them before they would come and take his belongings to his new address. If he didn't contact

Sour Face

them his belongings would remain in the house. They told me that I could arrange for his belongings to be sent to his new address or to a relative's house. This would not mean I was contacting him, so therefore I would not be interfering with his bail conditions.

That weekend two of my friends dropped his belongings off at his mother's house. They handed her a bag containing all of his personal documents, including his passport and the savings book proving that his half of the savings remained in the account. His mother was not impressed. She demanded to know the name of my friends, and was even less impressed when they wouldn't tell her.

"She can't do this", she shouted at them. "Packing all his belongings and sending them here. I haven't got the room to store them. I'm going to go down there and sort her out, once and for all". She never came.

The beating he gave me, that led to his arrested took place two weeks before we were due to go on holiday to India. He had chosen the itinerary, hotels, and arranged the transfers. I was going to pay for it out of my inheritance. Rather he said "We are going to pay for it out of the money that'll be in the savings account". He was very excited about this holiday, as India was a place he had always wanted to visit.

"You're very lucky to be going there. This is a holiday of a lifetime. Don't fucking expect to go away next year, because we won't be able to fucking afford it", he warned me.

It was strange, I never looked forward to this holiday, never got that buzz of excitement you have when you know you're going away.

Due to the circumstances there was no way I could go on holiday with him. I went to the local branch of the travel agents two days after he had attacked me to find out if there was any way I could cancel the holiday. My facial injuries were now extremely visible; my face was a mixture of different shades of blues and purples. I was very tearful. Every time someone spoke to me I felt the tears well up in my eyes. I asked if I could speak to the assistant who we had booked the holiday with. I had built up a rapport with her, whilst we were sorting out the details of the holiday. This person was the branch supervisor and she was wonderful. She took one look at me and whisked me away to a corner of the shop. I was in floods of tears as I explained to her, what had happened and how I needed to cancel this holiday. I wasn't bothered about getting any refund, but she was adamant that she would get me my half of the money back. She rang the travel insurance company who hadn't come across anyone who needed to cancel a holiday because their partner had beaten them up. They informed her that I needed a letter from my doctor stating I was not fit to travel. I would then get some of the money I had paid back. They would send the form to my home address. There was a problem. I wasn't living at that address; I was staying with my friends. Again the travel agent was fantastic, arranging for all correspondence to be sent to her at the travel agents. She would then send all correspondence to me at my workplace. The support and service I received from her was exceptional. I will never forget the kindness she showed towards me.

My GP gave his professional opinion that I was not medically fit to travel on a long haul flight. I received a cheque for almost half of the total cost of the holiday.

As part of the aftercare for domestic violence victims the police made weekly contact with me for three weeks. They referred me to the local domestic violence unit based in our local police station. I made an appointment and went to see my local domestic violence officer. It was the first time I'd ever been inside a police station. I was met by a WPC who worked for the domestic violence department. She was very professional and supportive. She advised me to change the locks on my front door, for my own safety, as I had been assessed as being a high-risk victim. This meant that if he harassed me at all and I rang the police giving them my home address, they would come immediately to where ever I was, as they considered me to be in great danger. She gave me the details of a local women's support group, where I could get legal advice regarding my house. A solicitor who specialized in domestic violence issues visited the group on a weekly basis. I rang the group and made an appointment to see the solicitor.

The local domestic violence support group had offices tucked away at the back of the town hall. A very pleasant woman who quickly put me at my ease met me. She ignored my obvious facial injuries, gave me forms to fill in and asked me if there was anything else the group could help me with. There wasn't but it was nice to know there was someone there if I did need any further help.

The solicitor I saw was extremely professional, asking me a succession of questions. He wanted fifteen thousand pounds as a settlement from the house. We had lived in the house for exactly six months before he was made to leave the house by the court. I had put twenty thousand pounds into the house as a deposit (he had insisted on that amount). We had a fixed rate mortgage for three years. This meant if the house were sold in this time we would have to give the building society five thousand pounds. Once legal fees were taken out of the equity this would leave twelve thousand pounds. Once this sum had been divided between two people, it would leave six thousand pounds each. The solicitor wanted to know how he arrived at fifteen thousand pounds being a fair settlement when he hadn't contributed anything to the deposit, I was the major wage earner, he had only lived in the house for six months and the reason we had split up was due to his violence. He has not and did not contribute anything towards the mortgage from the day he left.

"Due to the fact the money for the deposit and the items we brought for the house came out of our joint savings account. It sees it as our money", I replied.

"How did the money get into your savings account?" she asked me.

"I was left the money by an elderly relative" I

replied.

"Can you prove that?" was her next question.

"Yes I've got all the documents including solicitor's letters" I replied.

"My advice to you would be to stay in the house. Don't start any proceedings, as this will cost you in legal fees. Wait for him to contact you. Considering all the facts he certainly isn't entitled to fifteen thousand pounds, I would just offer him a good will gesture."

I was relieved by her advice but remained nervous about what would happen next. This was not going to be an easy situation to deal with.

I get angry when I think about how he wanted to rip me off .He wanted me to pay him for the privilege of beating me and abusing me for two years. During one of our last telephone conversations regarding the house settlement he said to me, "I was going to walk away with nothing. Let you keep the lot, but that's not fair to me".

I didn't reply.

I rang the bank explaining that the relationship had ended and that I needed to close the joint account. I was told to go into the local branch where someone would be able to help me. So I went into the local branch and explained what I wanted to do.

I was told that in order for the account to be closed, we both had to go into the bank.

I told them he no longer lived at my address and gave them his new address on a slip of paper.

The cashier refused to take it, as she informed me she could only take change of address from the customer concerned directly. Until he came in and told her he had moved all correspondence would continue to come to the address where we both had lived.

She went on to advise me to hand in my bankcard and chequebook for the account, which I did. I just wanted the stupid thing to be closed; I wanted nothing to do with the dam thing. The account would remain open until he also went into the bank and handed in his cash card.

"What happens if he doesn't comply?" I asked.

"Then the account will remain open. I'll put a note on the screen explaining that you have handed all the documentation relating to the account in to the bank", she replied.

"Could you write to him asking him to bring the bank card into this branch"? I was anxious to get the matter resolved.

"No I 'm sorry we can't get involved".

"What happens if he continues to use the account when there is no money in it and the account becomes overdrawn?" I asked.

"Then you will be legally responsible for half of the debt" was her reply.

"Even though you know I have no access to the account because I've just given you the cash card and cheque book? I was amazed.

"Yes. You are still responsible, because the account is open and you're name is on the account".

"But you won't let me close the dam account!" I was getting angry and frustrated.

Sour Face

"I have told you already. The account can't be closed until we have his bankcard, but if he overdraws on the account then you will be legally responsible for half of any debt that he accrues. Those are the rules of the bank".

I left the building feeling so worried and disillusioned with the whole banking system.

Two weeks later a bank statement arrived.

The account was two hundred and fifty pounds in arrears. I went back into the local branch and paid my half of the arrears, even though I had nothing to do with the account. I just didn't want to get in a financial mess.

The following month the bank statement told me that the account was now five hundred pounds in arrears. A letter demanding payment quickly followed this.

I rang the number on the letter.

I spoke to a very curt telesales person.

I explained to her again my situation.

"Yes, I can see from the screen that you have no access to the account and you haven't for four months. I can also see that you did pay half of the arrears on the account, but those arrears have gained interest that is why the amount due is now five hundred pounds."

"If I pay half of the arrears what will happen?" I asked

"That will fine, but we will still charge you interest on the remaining sum of money" was her reply.

"Will you contact him and tell him he owes this money, I have a forwarding address" I again asked her.

"We can't take that address from you, only he can

change his address details personally. Why don't you just ring him and tell him the situation". It was her turn to ask me questions now.

"No, I can't do that. I've been instructed by the court that I can't contact him due to the pending court case", I was getting so frustrated.

"Well we can't ring him. We can't get involved in domestic cases. We'll just continue to write to both of you regarding this debt at the address we have on record". Her voice was becoming sharp.

"But you know he doesn't live here", I was getting so frustrated.

"That doesn't matter. That is the address he gave us and until he personally tells us otherwise, that will remain his contact address".

"So will you continue to contact me and him at this address, threatening bailiffs and legal action until this amount is paid. Even though I have paid my half and you know he doesn't live here?"

"Yes" was the short answer.

"Well, I have to pay the whole amount then because you are not even going to try and contact him. It just seems so very unfair", my voice was shaking with emotion.

I gave her my bankcard details.

"Now can I close the account?" I asked her.

"No. You have been told. He has to go in and hand in his bankcard. Any arrears that accrue on the joint account you will be legally responsible for", she sounded annoyed with me.

"I want you to put on your stupid screen that I have paid those arrears myself. I also want you to note that you refused to accept any details of his whereabouts. If any letters come here to this address I will be forwarding them to his new address and I will see you in court because I refuse to pay another penny of his debt. I have never come across such an unfair unjust and ridiculous system in my entire life".

She hung up.

My hand was shaking as I replaced the telephone onto its stand. I was so upset, I cried for a long time.

As a recovering victim life is difficult enough without stupid rules making the situation ten times worse. I was bullied into paying all of those bank charges. If the account were in his name only the bank would want to know his forwarding address because they would want their money paid back. They didn't need his new address, not when they could steam roll me into paying all of the arrears. I am sure bullying victims of domestic violence who are willing to pay their half of any debt, but not all of a joint debt, is not included in any bank staff's training manual.

I did write to the chief executive of the bank, along with my local MP, informing them of my experiences. I also used the bank's complaints procedure and received a response.

I was told that they had followed their procedures and that they couldn't take his forwarding address from me to chase up his half of the debt due to these procedures. The address of our joint bank account quoted in the letter from them was his forwarding address. When I rang them to point this out and to find out why they hadn't contacted him regarding the arrears I was told that the person dealing with the complaint had left and the case was closed. I was told off the record that the bank had made mistakes when dealing with my case. But there was nothing further I could do.

The banking industry should feel ashamed of its self for treating vulnerable people in such an appalling way.

Sour Face

CHAPTER TEN

August bank holiday Monday we went to a carnival, organized by our local council. The day was sunny and warm. He appeared calm and settled. We'd had a fairly good day, watching various events and chatting. When we got back to the house he asked me what we would be having for tea. I replied that I didn't fancy cooking a proper meal, as I was tired. We'd been out all day. I suggested we had some items out of the freezer, or a take away meal. He began to give me a lecture,
" We're not having take- away food. It's too fucking expensive. You're spending money like water, I've told you, that you can't spend and save." "I don't want any of that fucking rubbish out of the freezer. That rubbish is fucking kid's food. I want proper food. Something with potatoes, I'm sick of you being so fucking lazy"
 I told him, that I didn't have time to cook a proper meal .It was now six o clock. If I started getting food ready, it would be really late by the time the meal would be cooked and even later by the time I'd washed up and cleaned the kitchen to his high standards. He started shouting at me.
"You are a fucking lazy bitch. I've never been with a woman as fucking lazy as you. The way you spend money like there's no tomorrow is just fucking ridiculous .We are not spending more money on food when you've already spent a fucking fortune on the shopping".
 I answered him back." No I'm not a bit lazy. I work dam hard in this house. I don't want to be

cooking all evening. I've got to go to work tomorrow. I want to relax. And another thing I don't over spend on anything. You won't let me".

He grabbed me by the neck, and I pushed his hands away. He then picked up the sofa I was sitting on, turned it on to its side, tipping me on to the floor. He then picked up the large sofa cushions and threw them at me, one after the other, followed by the cushions from the other sofa, small cushions from both of the sofas, and his shoes, keys, and television controls, one item after the other, all of them were aimed at my head. Slam.., Slam... slam.

"You answering back bitch. I've told you about fucking screaming at me, stupid fucking lazy whore". He shouted the words at the top of his voice.

I lay on the floor covering my head and face with my hands. He pulled my hands from my face, dragged me up from the floor by my arms, screaming in my face, his forehead against my forehead.

"Look at this fucking mess. Pick up all this fucking stuff. You always spoil everything. We can never go anywhere without you playing up when we get back. You always give me that sour face look."

I pulled the sofa back to its original position, against the wall, complete with all of the cushions. He told me sit down, which I did. He then carried on insulting me, asking me why I thought I had the right to answer him back.

"You should have defrosted the meat and prepared the potatoes before we went out this morning. Then all you would have had to do was put the gas on. Even you could manage to do that without complaining".

He came towards me. I remained sitting down, he straddled me, putting his knees either side of me on the sofa cushions. He grabbed my neck. This time the grabbing was different. He squeezed my windpipe with both hands, gripping it tighter and tighter. I couldn't get my breath. I began to panic and began to struggle.

I thought, "This is it. You're going to die". I fought unsuccessfully to get his hands away from around my neck. He then just let go of me. He got up off the sofa, and stood in front of me

"Did you think I was going to kill you? Were you scared?" he asked me.

Yes I did think he would kill me, and yes I was scared I replied.

He stared at me with a grin on his face "Yeah, I knew you were". He sat on the other sofa, turning the television on he said, "I'll go and get a pizza in a minute" without looking at me.

We went to Budapest for the bank holiday period. We were booked on the morning flight, so we were up very early. He began to get agitated, appearing very anxious. He began to find fault with everything about the prospective holiday. The flight times were inconvenient; the taxi firm wouldn't show up, our travel bags were too heavy. He began pacing the sitting room. I needed to get our coats out from the cupboard under the stairs, where we kept them. The morning was dark and cold. The previous few days had been very cold with wintery showers, which were forecasted to remain over Europe for the next five days. I took my cream wool coat out of the cupboard. I loved that coat. It was smart, fitted me well and had a hood with a fur trim. The hood kept my ears warm and my hair tidy. (I hate my ears being cold, and he would criticize my hair if it went fizzy in the rain). I didn't have to bother with using an umbrella, when wearing that coat. When he saw what coat I intended on taking with me, he was not at all happy.

"Why are you taking that fucking coat for? You know I fucking hate it."

I told him it was the only smart short coat I had, that I liked it, and it looked good with my jeans.

His reply "that's a winter coat. It's springtime. You should be wearing a jacket. Not that fucking thing. You'll look stupid and ugly if you go on holiday wearing that. Why don't you wear the other jacket?" The only other "jacket", I owned, was a lightweight, black, anorak type coat. It had a hole on the collar and was two sizes too big. I had meant to throw it away, when we moved in together. He knew that coat was in the cupboard; he wanted me to wear that one. He threw the other coat across the room.

"You are a stupid whore. You should make sure you have a decent jacket to wear when you're going away. It's not up to me to make sure you've got clothes".

I told him he didn't like me spending money on clothes, or indeed anything, without his permission.

He grabbed me by my neck, screaming in my face," cunt, sour face bitch. You've always upsetting me when we're going away. You always look a fucking mess".

He carried on throwing items around the sitting room, the cushions, books and the clothes out of the bags that were packed. Clothes fell everywhere. I was panicking. I picked the clothes up from the floor, repacking the bags as fast as I could; as the taxi was due to arrive at any minute. He stopped shouting and throwing things about.

He just stopped, saying he was "wound up, because we are going away."

I found myself apologising to him for not having the correct coat. I just wanted him to calm down, to stop being aggressive, and get into the taxi on time, so we wouldn't miss our flight. I ended up taking the lightweight jacket that was two sizes too big. I spent all of the holiday feeling extremely cold. He told me that I looked a mess because the coat was too big and my hair looked awful, as it rained all the time. I did have an umbrella with me, but he had to have that over his head, to stop his hair going frizzy in the rain. Whilst we were on holiday, we followed a walking tour of the city. The guidebook recommended a cafe in the main street. We went into the cafe, and because he wasn't happy with the prices in there he just stormed out, with me following him. That's the way it was. He'd walk off and I'd follow him, like a sheep. He stood in the middle of the street, shouting at me,

"For once I wish you stop staring at me with your fucking sour face. I'm not paying those ridiculous prices. Just because it's recommended in a guidebook doesn't mean its any good. You are so dim, you believe anything any fucker tells you", he mocked.

"I'm not dim". I answered back. "It seems like a nice place. We are on holiday. It would be nice to have a coffee in there."

"You are always thinking about your stomach. You are a gannet. You are always eating. That's why you are so fucking fat. You have had breakfast. That should be enough for the rest of the day. You really are a greedy cow".

"Its not that expensive and all I'd like is a drink. We don't have to eat anything", I replied.

"There are better places to have coffee. That place is a shit hole". He was ranting now.

"OK, we'll go where ever you want to go. Where is the nearest cafe?" I was doing my best to calm him down.

"I don't fucking know. You've got the guidebook. I just know there are cheaper places than that cafe. You have always got to spoil every trip we take by fucking answering me back. I 'm sick of telling you, you need to do as you're fucking told. I'm not having a cunt like you screaming at me".

"I'm fed up with you storming out of places leaving me standing on my own like an idiot. If you walk off again, I'm not following you. Give me the hotel key and I'll head back to the hotel". I stood in front of him.

"Fuck you", he replied, throwing the umbrella he was holding at my face. It hit me on the chin before falling onto the footpath. Turning from me in strode off in the direction we'd just come from.

I picked up the umbrella and returned to the hotel, where I sat in reception, until he came back.

Sour Face

He never mentioned the incident, just told me how he'd walked around the red light district where he'd seen "beautiful looking whores",
"I thought it would be fun to find the sex part of town. Every city has one. I like looking at all of the whores waiting to get a man, all desperate for some cock" .He smiled at those images.
"They really look after themselves. Some of them are your age and they look really good, better than you do. They have fantastic bodies, not great big stomachs like you've got. You are so fat. It's all that food you keep on eating. You should only have one meal a day. That's all you need."
I ignored him.
"I slept with a prostitute when I went to Berlin with my mates. She was beautiful, the best looking one in the nightclub. She was from Poland. East European women are so gorgeous."
"I thought you had a girl friend when you went there", I was surprised at his admission.
"Yes I did, but she was a silly cow. I knew that relationship wasn't going anywhere. She acted like she was the boss. She thought she was in control of me. As if I'm going to let a fucking woman ever be in control of me. She was more intelligent than you. She worked part time in a butcher's shop and used to give me free bacon and sausages to take home. She was beautiful and she loved me very much. I loved fucking her". He looked directly at my face for a reaction.
"So if everything was so wonderful with her, why did you feel there was a need to sleep with a prostitute?" I asked him. "What did your girlfriend think about that?"

"Never fucking told her. I do want I want when I want. All of the lads slept with whores that weekend. I went to see her when I got back from Berlin. I brought her a diamond and white gold bracelet. She was made up with it. Fucking should have been. Cost over two hundred pounds, I didn't mean to spend that much, I just wanted to impress her. We went out and we got back I fucked her. It's what she wanted, what all women want from me. She told me I was the best lover she ever had. We both know that's true"

The very last holiday we had together was in mainland Spain. Two weeks together. He was always agitated when he was away. He felt that people were watching him. He also drank a lot. As most people do on holiday. The only thing with him was that he didn't know when to stop drinking once he'd started. He knew when I should stop and would watch what I was drinking. He hated me drinking cocktails, which I love when I'm on holiday. He thought they made me a loud drunk, and turned me into his mother. I had to drink diet coke whilst he carried on getting more and drunk. That sounds resentful, and yes I was, very resentful. I couldn't be myself. I had to be what he wanted me to be, the perfect woman. I wanted to be like normal couples that were on holiday. I would see them, walking around hand in hand, laughing with each other, sharing jugs of cocktails, generally having a really nice time, together. I wanted to have that so much. I really tried to create that with him, but he didn't want it. He did what he wanted when he wanted, and if I didn't

Sour Face

like it then I could fuck off. I wish I'd had a pound for every time I'd heard those words during our two years together. I know it's a cliché, but I would be a very rich woman indeed.

One evening, during the first week of our holiday, we went out for a meal. We had a nice time, chatting and drinking wine. That was the way; the evenings usually went when he was in a good mood. We went to a local bar where he began talking to an English man who had settled in the resort. He brought lots of drinks for this man and his friends. He drank a large amount of beer. I sat next to him, with my diet coke, while he played the nice charming man to his audience, watching him getting extremely drunk. He began arguing with me as soon as we left the bar. He was very annoyed with me. We reached our hotel room. He refused to go to bed instead he sat on the balcony shouting at me. It was two o' clock in the morning. I tried to calm him down, to make him stop shouting. Instead I made him worse.

"Who are you stupid bitch?" "I've told you. No one tells me what to do".

He stood in the doorway, between the hotel room and the balcony. He grabbed me by my neck, he walked forwards, pushing me backwards, still holding onto my neck, and he slammed my back against the wall. A large mirror hung on this wall. I caught my head on the frame, as my head hit the wall. I began to cry. I just couldn't help it. It was really painful. He let go of my neck, grabbing my hair with both of his hands; he threw me on to the bed.

All the time, shouting at me."Whore, tart, cunt,

you are a stupid sour face bitch".

Holding back my tears, I whispered to him, trying so hard to get him to stop shouting, reminding him that there were people next door to us. He went back onto the balcony, muttering to himself, with a bottle of beer from the mini bar for company. Within ten minutes he was asleep, in the chair on the balcony. I crept out of the hotel room. Wrapped up in a blanket, I sat on the stairs of the fire escape, crying. I was so upset. Wondering when this behaviour would stop. When would he learn to behave rationally and become a "normal" person? I know now he never will. Back then I did think he would change. We just needed to get this situation or that situation over with and he would be settled. The amount of excuses I made for him. What a waste of my time and energy that was.

The next morning he told me he couldn't remember any of the previous night's events. I told him that the family next door would probably complain about the noise that had come from our room. (There were two women next door with their children).

His reply was "Do you think I care about any bastard tarts. Let them come round and talk to me if they've got something to say".

We walked past them, in the corridor on the way to the dining room. They stared at us and spoke in low voices during breakfast. This unnerved him. He was edgy, anxious.

He repeatedly asked me "what is their fucking problem? Do they want a piece of me or what? I don't care about them".

But he did care. He always cared about what

Sour Face

people thought about him. He wanted to be liked. The family didn't complain. The hotel management said nothing to us. We didn't go to breakfast for the next three days.

His reason being he was "sick of that crap they keep on giving us".

When the family next door went home, we began to eat breakfast in the hotel again.

The first New Year we spent together, Matt and Bernie had arranged to go to a local club, on New Year's Eve. He'd arranged for us to go to our local pub, which was within walking distance of this club. As it was New Years Eve, our local pub was charging a five-pound entrance fee. His friends were going to be there, so was Jill and Darren. About ten o'clock, Jill and Darren announced that they would also be going to the club. I really wanted to go so badly. This would be the first time in a few years that I would be able to spend New Year's Eve with my Children. I asked him if we could go.

"No. We've already paid five fucking pounds to come in to our local pub. We both know that's a fucking rip off. I'm not paying any more fucking money to go to that shit hole".

"Please could we go just for an hour "I pleaded with him" I really want to see Matt and Bernie. It's New Years Eve. It would mean so much to me. If we go there tonight I won't go out next week, I'll stay at home so we won't be spending any extra money".

"No we are not fucking going. None of my friends are going down there. We're staying here and that's it". He left me and returned to his group of male friends.

He wouldn't be persuaded so Jill and Darren went without me, leaving me to stand with him and his friends. He was very annoyed with me for wanting to change his plans. He was verbally aggressive and abusive towards me, whilst smiling. He would lean into me; spitting words of abuse in my face, then look up throw his head back and laugh like he was joking with me. I would get upset. People standing around us would think I was being teary and "difficult/neurotic", because that is what they could see. He'd created that illusion by his staged behaviour. He remained abusive for about an hour and a half. When I could no longer tolerate his abuse, I walked out of the pub just before midnight. He followed me outside and we argued in the taxi car park.

He ignored me for the next day, after he'd told me; "You were so out of fucking order last night. All my mates couldn't believe what a fucking whore you are and how you were playing up. All this fuss over wanting to spend time with your fucking spoilt kids. I wouldn't care but they don't give a fuck about you. You really are fucking pathetic. You need to fucking apologise to me now for being such an evil cunt".

He made me apologise for my behaviour and for spoiling his New Years Eve. I did apologise to him. But I didn't mean any of the words. I just did it to pacify him.

One Saturday he was in a foul mood. It was his day off and he was very hung over. I wasn't quick

Sour Face

enough in getting his breakfast ready and he was very impatient.

"Hurry up bitch. What are you fucking doing in there, killing the fucking pig"? He shouted from the hallway.

He went into the sitting room and slammed the door so hard that the handle fell off and he was trapped inside. He was not a bit happy.

"Fucking hell! I'm trapped inside this fucking room. You fucking bitch this is your entire fault. If my breakfast was ready I wouldn't have had to come out and see what was happening".

Bits of the handle were on the floor in the hall.

All that was visible in the actual door was the inside mechanisms of the door lock.

I stood outside of the door giggling I couldn't help it. I thought "Thank you. There is someone watching out for me after all".

"Where are you fucking bitch?"

"I'm outside the door. Are you Ok?" I asked him stifling my laughter.

"Of course I'm not OK you silly bitch .I'm locked in this fucking room. The door handle is in pieces all over the fucking floor, and I can't get fucking out!" He was ranting now.

The more frustrated he got the funnier I found the situation.

"Shall I ring for the fire brigade?" I suggested from the kitchen. I couldn't help myself the laughter was now coming over me in waves. I had to go from the hall or he would have heard me.

"No! Don't fucking ring them I'll be a laughing stock, Get me the red screwdriver from the toolkit. Pass it me through the window. Hurry up "he shouted.

I went outside and past him the screwdriver through the window, trying so hard not to laugh. He was standing in the middle of the room, his face red with temper. He grabbed the screwdriver from me and went to the door.

Shouting instructions to me from the other side of the door he managed to fix the handle and finally got out of the room. He had been locked inside for over half an hour. Once he was out of the room he spent a further half an hour checking the door, handle and door frame.

He never slammed that door shut again.

The last New Year we spent together we were supposed to have dinner with his best friend and his partner at their flat. We had then arranged to meet our other friends at our local pub later that evening.

Early in the afternoon, his friend telephoned to cancel, as his partner was not well, and there had also been some problem arranging a baby sitter.

He was not happy that his plans had been changed.

"He's a fucking bastard. He calls himself a mate and then does this to me", he shouted.

"He can't help it if his partner is not very well", I replied. "It would have been nice to see them, but we can do that another time. We'll just meet up with our other friends earlier. We'll still have a nice evening."

"Go out on your fucking own. I'm not going. I haven't any friends since I've been living with you".

Sour Face

"I can't go out on my own on New Year's Eve. Look I'm really sorry if your friend has upset you, but he's upset you, I haven't. Ring him and tell him that he's upset you, don't tell me there's nothing I can do about the situation. "I tried to reason with him.

"I'm not going to ring that stupid bastard. He's too under the thumb; he always does what she tells him to do. He's a fucking idiot. I'm not going out either. It's up to you what you decide to do", he replied.

"Don't be stupid", I tried to reason with him. "Don't let this spoil our New Year".

"Don't call me stupid, you fucking sour face bitch. How fucking dim are you? What in the words I am not going out don't you understand? I am too fucking upset to go out tonight. I told you go on your fucking own. I am not going anywhere and that's fucking final."

The last time I'd gone out by myself I had been physically abused on my return. I didn't want that to happen again. I rang Jill and made the excuse that he wasn't feeling very well, so I couldn't leave him on his own on New Year's Eve. She was upset at the change of our plans at such short notice. She wished me a Happy New Year.

We spent the evening in the sitting room. I had placed a basket of sweets under the Christmas tree that evening. I hadn't eaten any of them. When I looked in the basket it was empty.

"Where have all the chocolates gone?" I asked him.

"I've eaten them. I thought that is what they were for, me to eat. Didn't realise they were for fucking show."

"There was a whole large box of chocolates in that basket. I haven't had one of them", I was amazed that anyone could eat so many chocolates in such a short space of time.

"That's your own fucking fault. I haven't stopped you having any. You should have had some earlier", he replied sarcastically.

He lay on one sofa with his back to me. He refused to speak to me, look at me or have a glass of wine with me. He remained like that all evening.

The chimes of Big Ben striking midnight peeled out from the television. The flash of fireworks from outside filled the sitting room with light.

He remained lying on the sofa pretending to be asleep.

I wished him a "Happy New Year".

He ignored me.

I was very upset. Feeling extremely alone I went upstairs to bed. About ten minutes later he joined me. He lay in the bed, with his back towards me, as far as physically possible away from me. He quickly went to sleep. I woke the next morning to find that the large space in between us remained.

CHAPTER ELEVEN

I am a very healthy person. One Monday I felt very sick and vomited several times at work. I telephoned him to let him know I wasn't well and that I would be leaving work at three o' clock. I went straight to bed I was still in bed when he returned from work.

"How are you now"? He asked me from the doorway of the bedroom. "Have you been sick again?"

"No but I still feel really rough", I replied.

"You're not going to stay in fucking bed are you? There's no need to be in fucking bed if you're not vomiting. Get up. I'm fucking starving". He began to shout.

"I can't face cooking tonight. There is some bolognaise in a bowl in the fridge already made. All you need to do is warm it in the microwave and put some pasta to boil in a saucepan of water". I felt very nauseous.

"I can't be bothered to fucking cook anything. I don't want to be fucking messing about with fucking pasta and fucking saucepans. "Get up out of fucking bed now, or I'll drag you out", he demanded.

I got up out of the bed, putting on my dressing gown, "Then ring for a take away, there is no way I can cook for you tonight".

"I'm not spending money on fucking take away food. You are so fucking lazy. You don't care that I've been to work all day. You haven't been sick for hours. There is nothing fucking wrong with you lazy cunt".

I went into the kitchen and started getting his tea ready. The smell of cooking filled the kitchen. Within ten minutes I'd vomited. I carried on vomiting for as long as it took me to prepare his meal. He sat in the sitting room watching television. I took his tea into him on a tray.
"I'm going back to bed", I told him.
"You look fucking awful. Your breath stinks. I didn't ask you to cook for me; you enjoy being the martyr so much. I'm not washing up. I told you I don't do anything domestic. Where shall I leave the plates", he asked me with his mouth full of food.
"Put them in the bottom part of the dishwasher and I'll sort them out tomorrow ", were my parting words, as I went back up the stairs to bed.

I was having gynaecological problems. My GP arranged for me to have an operation to rectify this. This would mean I would have to go into hospital, as a day case. I would go in the morning and return home the same afternoon.

The morning of the operation, following the instructions sent to me by the hospital, I had a shower, washed my hair and out on clean comfortable clothing. I had chosen a pink long sleeved t-shirt top and a black pair of pull on type trousers. These would be easy to put on after the surgery.
He stared at me "you look like a fucking old woman. You look fucking stupid".
"I don't care what I look like", I was annoyed with him "I'm going to hospital not for a night on the

Sour Face

town".

"Fucking sour face bitch, you can't help yourself can you? You have to answer me back", he shouted at me.

Moving towards me he grabbed me by the neck and dragged me into the corner of the room.

"I hate you, you fucking old sour face bitch", he screamed in my face. "You always look such a fucking mess, like a fucking tramp".

He let go of my neck. Looking at me with a smirk on his face he asked me" are you nervous about this operation?"

"Yes I am, and the last thing I need now is for you to behave like this. I've got to be there by seven forty five I'll miss the bus if you won't let me go". I was trying so hard to keep calm, trying not to cry.

"I've not done anything wrong. You shouldn't have shouted me. I can't believe you are nervous about a simple little operation. You really are a fucking wimp. I'm not stopping you leaving. Go on fuck off. I'll see you later". He left the sitting room and went into the kitchen.

Grabbing my backpack, I pulled on my coat and went out of the house without saying goodbye to him.

I was anxious and nervous as I waited for the bus; I managed to compose myself by the time I reached the day unit of the local hospital.

The operation went well. I was told to take a month off sick from work. This wasn't possible, as I would only be paid for one week's salary from work.

"We can't afford for you to be off fucking work. You'll be all right. It's not like you do fucking hard work, you sit on your fat arse all day", he had said when I told him the amount of time the GP had informed me I would need off after the operation.

I spoke to the surgeon after the surgery. He reluctantly gave me a sick note for one week on the condition that I did light part time duties for my first few weeks back at work.

My blood pressure was taken. The reading was very low so I was advised to drink several glasses of water, which I did. This improved my blood pressure reading and I was fit for discharge.

He came into the cubicle.

"You look really well", were his opening words "You can come home; they told me that you're fine".

He never mentioned the events of that morning.

I felt awful. I looked pale, the wound area was sore, and I found it difficult to get dressed as I was advised not to bend or stretch for at least four weeks. He stood in the cubicle watching me as I struggled to get dressed.

"Can you get my bag out of the locker please I can't reach it" I asked him.

"They told me you were all right to be discharged. Don't use this operation as an excuse to be even more fucking lazy than usual", was his reply as he handed me my bag, leaving me to pack my things.

We had a chat with the nurse before we left the unit. She told him he wasn't to leave me alone for forty-eight hours. I was to do no bending or stretching for four weeks, and to be careful with stairs and not to make too many unnecessary journeys. She gave me a box of painkillers and told me to take them every four hours.

Sour Face

When we reached home I was exhausted. He had taken two days off work, as I couldn't be left on my own. I had cooked meals and frozen them before I went into hospital. I had put the food into disposable plastic containers. All he had to do was to defrost them and warm the food in the microwave. He'd have to wash up the plates for at least the first two days. I thought that if he didn't wash up, then I would only have a few plates to deal with not a sink full of dishes, which I could easily do when I was well enough to potter about.

I wanted to go to bed. I felt tired and very rough.

"You look fine, there's nothing wrong with you. There's no need to go to fucking bed. Lie on the sofa if you have to", he said. "I don't want you upstairs."

The effort to walk up and down the stairs was awesome. I got changed into my pyjamas and went and lay on the sofa propped up with pillows.

After about ten minutes I began to feel nauseous.

"Can you get me the bucket from under the sink, in the kitchen? I feel like I'm going to be sick" I asked him.

"You look fine to me. Stop being a fucking martyr", he replied.

I dragged myself off the sofa and went to collect the bucket and a box of tissues.

I began to vomit at about four thirty. By nine thirty I was still vomiting. I was having a reaction to the anaesthetic. I was in a lot of pain but was unable to take any painkillers due to the vomiting.

He began shouting at me from the second time I was sick.

"You look awful. Stop being sick, you're doing it on

fucking purpose to get me to feel sorry for you".

"I'm really sorry. I can't help it honestly", I replied in between vomits.

"Look at you. Stop heaving when I'm talking to you", he shouted coming towards me.

I began to vomit again.

He kicked my legs while I was vomiting." You fucking sour face bitch. I'll make you stop being fucking sick", he shouted. He then grabbed my shoulders and shook me whilst I continued to be sick.

Vomit went all over my clothing and onto the carpet.

I began to cry. I was frightened, in pain and I couldn't cope with his aggression.

"If you won't stop being sick, I suppose I'd better ring the fucking doctor ", he said as I cleaned up the vomit from the floor. " This is just fucking great. I suppose we'll end up in the fucking hospital all night long".

The GP came to visit within half an hour of telephoning. He explained that I was having a reaction to the anaesthetic. He gave me an injection and told me if I didn't stop vomiting I would have to go back into hospital, as I would suffer from dehydration. He checked the wound, which was clean and dry, advised me to go to bed, rather than stay on the sofa and to telephone again if there were any further problems.

Once I settled in bed I did manage to get to sleep.

The next morning when I woke up I was still feeling very nauseous.

"How are you now", he asked me.

"I feel sick" I replied.

Sour Face

"Not again. I cant' put up with this for the fucking days I'm off work", he shouted.

I was sick, as soon as I woke up, but that was the only time that day.

I remained very tired and wanted to stay in bed. He wouldn't let me.

"Get up, fucking lazy bitch. You fucking stink of sweat and vomit. Your hair looks like fucking string. I can't bear to smell you, god, it's a stench." He waved his hand in front of his nose.

I struggled downstairs and climbed in and out of the shower.

I was so very tired. I had no energy at all .He made himself drinks and ate the food I had prepared and stored in the freezer. He refused to do any housework or load the washing machine, leaving the dirty laundry in a pile on the kitchen floor for me to sort out when I was well enough.

"You'll be alright tomorrow. You can sort out all those jobs then. I'm on holiday from work. I'm not spending my holiday doing fucking housework", he informed me.

When he took annual days from work, he spent the time doing exactly what he wanted to do. He would spend the day in bed, watch DVD's, or read. I would return from work to find him sitting in his t – shirt and boxer shorts, in front of the television. He wouldn't get up and make us a hot drink. He would wait for me to take my coat off and then ask me to make a drink. This would be followed by "What are you making for tea? I'm starving. I couldn't be bothered making any fucking food. You should leave me a sandwich in the fridge for lunchtime. You can make it before you go to work". I would ignore him and go into the kitchen. If he were in a good mood he would suggest that we have a take away meal for our evening meal. He would never offer to cook or make a sandwich.

I resented the way he was allowed to have time off to do what he wanted. I was never allowed that luxury. When I took any annual leave I was expected to get up the same time as I did for work. I would get his breakfast, and prepare his lunch for him to take to work, then begin the list of tasks he had prepared for me. These would include, cleaning the door knobs with brass polish, dusting the door frames and skirting boards, weeding outside in the gardens, tidying out various cupboards, and cleaning the inside of every kitchen cupboard. He would lecture me about how these tasks needed doing, as the house was "filthy". He would constantly remind me that I needed to maintain the house in the high standards that he expected. It was just easier to do the stupid housework, rather than argue with him. At least I knew when he came home from work he would be in a settled frame of mind if my cleaning met his inspection. I learnt over time what areas he would check, such as the corners of the room. I would clean these first and then put the furniture back, without cleaning any further. He never found out.

The following day I did feel better, and that was the end of my convalescence period. He went back to sitting around with me waiting on him as I usually did. The only thing was that I really couldn't physically do a great deal as I didn't have the energy, my body wouldn't let me do what I usually did. After each job, even making the tea, I would find I would have to sit down and rest for a while before I could do any further tasks.

He decided that because it was Friday he was going out with his friends. He felt I was well and healthy, so there was no need to stay in the house with me.

"I can't stay indoors all day and all night, it drives me mad. I used to do that all the time when I was married because we never had any money to go anywhere", he said, "You'll be alright if I go out. You'll go to fucking bed anyway".

Jill and Darren came around that evening, and we had a pleasant time, chatting and drinking tea. They left early, and I went to bed, as I was still very tired.

He came back about two o'clock. He woke me up by his usual shaking of my shoulders.

"I'm fucking starving .is there anything to eat in this fucking place?" he asked me.

"I've left you some sandwiches on a plate in the kitchen", I replied still half asleep.

"Good ". He sat on the side of the bed.

"I've had a fucking great time. We went to this club that was full of older women. It was like Christmas. I didn't know which way to turn. We pulled two women. They were gorgeous. She wanted to see me again. I told her that I lived with someone. She wanted me to go home with her for sex. She said I could stay until the morning. I told her I was not interested in having sex with her, even though she was very attractive. I won't do anything to jeopardise my relationship with you. I certainly wouldn't do so by having sex with some dirty whore".

He got into bed with all his clothes on. He carried on talking about his evening for the next half an hour until he fell asleep.

The next day he carried on the conversation about the woman he was chatting to the previous night. We were in the kitchen. He was watching me making his breakfast.

"She was really coming onto me. She wanted me very much", he boasted.

"You told me about her last night. I don't really want to hear it again this morning", I told him as I turned the bacon over.

It was three days after the operation. Severe bruising was now evident across my abdomen and into both groins. I felt very unattractive and my general mood was low. The last thing I needed was for him to tell me about his conquests with very attractive women.

He stood in front of me. "You're fucking jealous. I can't stand fucking jealous women", he shouted.

"I'm not jealous. Obviously something happened last night with this woman. You can't stop talking about her. "I was exhausted with the entire situation. I couldn't cope with his insensitivity.

"I can't believe that you would think I would be unfaithful", he shouted. Moving closer he grabbed me by the neck and slammed me against the kitchen wall.

Holding me by the neck he shouted. "You are a fucking jealous sour face cunt. I haven't done anything to harm this relationship. If you don't believe that then you can just fuck off". He let go

Sour Face

of me and returned to the sitting room, muttering about how he couldn't understand how unreasonable I was being. I carried on with cooking his breakfast, taking to him when it was ready for him to eat.

He wanted to have sex that afternoon, because it was Saturday. We always had sex on a Saturday afternoon, as he was either a day off from work, or had finished at lunchtime. I couldn't have sex with him. I was very sore from the operation I'd had three days ago. He was not happy.

"Are you fucking refusing me sex, fucking bitch?" he demanded.

"I can't have sex with you. It's a physical impossibility. Have you seen the extent of the bruising"? I asked him.

"I'm not fucking looking at that. It's fucking horrible ", he answered.

He decided that if he couldn't have sex with me, he would masturbate over me. He then ejaculated over my stomach, making sure that the wound area was covered with my white lace knickers, so he wasn't able to see any of the wound or bruising. Afterwards he fastened his jeans, and without looking at me he told me "I'm going for a lie down upstairs. I'm fucking knackered". He left me sitting on the sofa, my abdomen still covered with his bodily fluid. I felt so degraded and dirty. I hobbled to the bathroom where I cleaned myself and changed into clean clothing.

On Sunday I was expected to cook a full Sunday lunch. Afterwards I was expected to wash up and clean the kitchen to his usual high standards. This whole procedure took an hour and a half. I had to keep on resting in between the household tasks. This included bending and stretching, but what could I do? No one else was going to help me. I was exhausted by the time I had finished. During this time he remained lying on the sofa in the sitting room, eventually nodding off to sleep. He woke about six o'clock asking me "What are you making for tea I'm fucking starving".

At the very beginning of our relationship, we were in bed chatting.
He had told me he had had many lovers; he certainly appeared very sexually experienced.
He asked me, "am I the best lover you've ever had?"
This would be a frequently asked question throughout our relationship.
I didn't want to upset him or make him feel bad about himself.
"Yes, you are". I replied
"There is a definite chemistry between me and you, but you aren't the best lover I've had. It's hardly swinging from the chandeliers sex. I've had a lot more adventurous sex with other women". He looked at me. He was being deadly serious.
"Well, I can't be good at everything", I tried to make a joke of the situation.
"That's what I don't understand about you. Whatever I say to you about other women you don't get jealous", He looked puzzled.
"What is the point of getting jealous about events that happened before you met me? Is that why

Sour Face

you tell me about past girlfriends? Do you what me to be jealous?" I was curious.

"My wife was very jealous about my ex girlfriends. It showed she cared enough about me to give me a reaction. It makes you appear a fucking cold fish, when there is not even a spark of jealously from you".

"I'm afraid that's my nature. I'm not a jealous person, and I'm not going to change. In my opinion jealously isn't a very nice trait to have. You should be grateful that I don't give you a hard time regarding your past. Doesn't it make a refreshing change?" I asked him.

"It's fucking different, I suppose. May be you'll change as our relationship grows", he suggested.

"We'll see", I replied, knowing full well that this would not be the case.

I turned to him and asked him "So tell me then, have you any sex secrets to tell me?"

"Well I did have sex with my mother's best friend, twice. I really fancied her. She was gorgeous, had fantastic legs. She wanted us to carry on seeing each other, but that couldn't happen. My mother would have killed her. She doesn't know. No one else in the family knows about it".

"Have you ever had sex with any of your relatives?" He was deadly serious.

The look on my face showed him that I was stunned by this question.

"No I haven't. I couldn't think of anything more horrible", I was horrified by the suggestion.

"Stop being Miss Prim. Are you sure you've got nothing to tell me? Remember we promised to be completely honest with each other there's nothing wrong with a bit of incest. Are you sure nothing happen with any male relative? Not even a kiss or a grope with any of them?"

"No, I've told you that nothing like that ever happened to me. We are a normal caring family". I was shelled shocked at his views that incest was acceptable.

"OK, calm down it was only a question. I didn't mean to upset you ". His apology appeared sincere.

"That's OK. I asked the question", I replied.

"Have you anything else to tell me? Have you any sexual fetishes?" I was joking. I was trying to lighten the mood.

You can imagine my surprise when he answered, "Yes, I do".

"Are you serious, or are you winding me up?"I could tell by the look on his face that he wasn't joking.

"Don't judge me. You asked the question and I've been honest with you".

"What is it then?"

"I have a harmless fetish. I like tights", he replied, looking straight into my face for any signs of a reaction." I've always liked women in tights from being a young boy. I really like tall women, with really long legs, turns me on".

"Yes it sounds harmless. I know men get turned on by stockings, so tights are just a variation of them". I was relieved. After his admission about his sexual conquest with his mother's best friend, I was prepared for anything.

"I love seeing the young girls going to school with their little short checked skirts on and their natural

Sour Face

tights. It turns me on. I'd love to fuck a school girl".
Again he looked at me for a reaction, with a smile on his face.
"No you don't you're just trying to get a reaction out of me. We both know that you like older not younger women. That's because older women make a fuss of you and look after you."
I was trying to distract him. My tactics worked. The thought of him being serious made my blood run cold, not out of any kind of jealously but out of repulsion. It remains a nasty vile thought he would have sexual desires or fantasy's regarding young teen-age girls.
Following his admission of his fetish, he introduced tights into our sexual relationship. Rather they became his focus of our sexual relationship.
He would buy them for me and bring them home for me to wear. He would know the denier of the tights by putting his hand inside the leg part and then rub them across his cheek. He only liked to buy fifteen- denier and had certain colours of tights that he would buy, American tan being his favourite.
I discovered that he didn't like me wearing trousers, because when I wore a skirt it would guarantee I would wear tights. He didn't like me choosing my tights for work; he insisted that he brought every pair of tights that came into my house. He would get very sexually aroused when purchasing the tights. This was the main reason he liked to go and buy them for me.
"You buy some fucking horrible colours and they're too fucking thin", he would shout at me,

"you know I hate those fucking dark colours you buy".
"They are just something I put on my legs to stop them getting cold. You are taking this tight thing a bit too far". I was annoyed with him.
"Don't fucking mock me you stupid bitch. Stop fucking screaming at me, I 've told you I won't have you treating me that way".
As usual I found myself apologising for my behaviour.

He liked me to wear tights for him during sex. He told me that his wife had done this for him, so had all of this other girl friends. It was expected by him that I would do the same.
This phrase "to wear tights for him", meant to wear tights whilst we had sex.
In an adult relationship, many women dress up for their partners. This makes them feel attractive and adds excitement to a loving caring relationship.
This was not the case in this situation.
He would not have sex with me unless I was wearing tights, with white lace knickers on underneath them.
He would get his satisfaction by ripping the panty part of the tights, before we had sex. And that was what it was sex, not loving making. There was never any loving foreplay such as stroking each other's bodies. Everything was about his sexual gratification. I the person wasn't what he was having sex with. He was getting his satisfaction from the tights, anyone could have been wearing them, and the end results for him would be the same.

Sour Face

He would regularly visit tight porn web sites on the Internet. I never knew such places existed until I saw him looking at them. These sites involved younger men having sex with older women. All of the women in the videos wore tights. He would masturbate in front of the computer screen and then call me to show me what he was watching. He would expect me to sit next to him, whilst we both watched the computer monitor. The whole process was very graphic and clinical, which I suppose all porn is. He would tell me to "go and put your fucking tights on, fucking whore". He would then want sex whilst watching the computer porn. I was just an extension of the porn, my body a vessel in which to satisfy him. My needs were not important. In fact they were nonexistent.

He would also expect me to pose for him wearing short skirts tights and lace under ware. He would then take pictures of me with his mobile phone. I never found out if he had shown those pictures to anyone.

He would call me names constantly when we had sex: bitch, whore, slut, and tart usually. He also liked to call me Mum, or Mummy. I was appalled and shocked by this behaviour. He got very turned on by the thought of incest, particularly by a son having sex with their mother. This was the reason he liked American tan tights so much, they reminded him of the dinner ladies from the school he attended as a young boy.

Once we were living together he never told me he loved me during sex.

We never had sex with either of us naked. Even when we went on holiday abroad, I had to pack boxes of tights.

He would also like to wear tights himself. He would always buy American tan tights, fifteen-denier in a large size, for him to wear. He would wear them under his jeans when we went out shopping and would get very aroused by this. The first time I saw him in his tights I was gob smacked.

He told me "This is what I do. There is no harm in it. I've worn them with all of my previous girl friends and they accepted it."

He also liked to wear my knickers, and actually brought himself a pair of his own white lace knickers, as mine were too small for him.

I came home from work one day to find him sitting on the sofa dressed in his tights, white lace knickers, and my black satin waist under skirt. He was masturbating. I tried not to look shocked.

"I found this in your drawer. I like it, makes me feel sexy. Come here, I've been waiting for you to get back. I want to fuck you", he demanded.

So we had sex. We always had sex when he wanted it. He never liked me to get changed out of my work clothes when I came home. He wanted me to keep my skirt and tights on until I went to bed, in case he wanted sex that evening.

He would sometimes have sex with me whilst he wore tights. He would like me to feel his legs in the tights whilst we had sex. It was the most bizarre thing I have ever done in my life.

He would call me into the sitting room from the kitchen.

"I'm fucking horny, bitch", he said, masturbating in front of me. "Sit down over there and lift you're

Sour Face

fucking skirt up, I'm going to fetch over you, fucking whore".

This meant he would ejaculate over the bodice part of the tights. Throughout this process he would focus on the tights, calling me his usual names.

After his orgasm, he would look at me, with disgust "you need to go and fucking clean yourself up. Make sure you don't get any fucking mess on the floor". He would then carry on watching television.

I personally have no sexual hang ups. What two consenting adults do in the privacy of their own homes is fine by me. That word is the key to the entire situation: consenting. In a controlled abusive relationship does the victim really consent? I did what pleased him, my abuser, but in the relationship, I didn't see him as that. I saw him as my partner that I wanted to please I wanted to make him happy. I was so conditioned. I really believed that satisfying all of his needs was my purpose in life.

If I didn't do as he wanted I knew that there would be consequences. I was made to feel so insecure that he would leave me if I didn't grant him his sexual rights.

For him sex was all about his control over me, in order to fulfil his desires and needs.

A survey of 1,236 women living in London (Hall 1985), found that 9% of the women questioned had at sometime been forced to have sex by their partner. This is the only piece of research I have been able to find on this subject.

Finkelhar and Yello (1988) categorised an

"obsessive rapist". They use this category to describe a martial rapist who is found to have bizarre and or perverse sexual interests. This occurs in 10% of martial rapists. The perpetrator's only sexual act is the fulfilling of his sexual interest, and the victim is forced into taking part.

There are ways of making someone have sex without physically forcing them to.

I felt degraded, unloved and so ashamed after each time we had sex.

I wanted to be loved and respected. I wanted to feel special, to have someone call me by my real name. I wanted someone to be making love to me, the person, without any specific clothing of any kind.

I thought that respect and love during sex were fantasy stereotypes created by the media. I believed this has I had never experienced any of this in my life.

Over the years I was conditioned into believing that what we did was harmless and "real". He talked about how real our relationship was all the time.

He told me that for the first time in his life he didn't have to pretend with a woman. He could be himself and behave just as he had always wanted to. I would put up with his sexual behaviour because I really loved him. By him making these types of statements he was increasing the emotional control over me. I was convinced that I did love him, so I would tolerate our sex life to demonstrate this to him. I had confused traumatic bonding with feelings of love. The more research I do on the subject and the more I examine my own

Sour Face

relationship deepens my belief that I was a victim of traumatic bonding. I wasn't in love with him.

If I tried to introduce any normality or kindness into any areas of our relationship, I would be mocked.

"Stop looking at life through fucking rose tinted glasses. This is real life, not a fucking novel, you need to come down from your ivory tower and join the real world".

He would tell anyone that he never physically forced me to have sex. He didn't need to. His emotional and mental control over me ensured that I would do as he said.

CHAPTER TWELVE

Two days after the bind over order was in place he telephoned. I was at my work place.
"How are you?" he asked.
My heart leapt at the sound of his voice.
"I'm alright. What do you want?"
"There's no need to be hostile. I want to know what you intend to do about the house. Legally it's half mine. I need ten thousand pounds as soon as possible as I want to leave the area."
I was shocked, at the thought of him going away. I composed myself" anything to do with the house needs to go through the legal system".
"I know that. I don't care about the house. I care about you. I miss you". He sounded sincere.
"Please don't say that, "I wasn't prepared for this admission of feelings.
"I'm telling the truth. I do miss you, so much. I'm sorry for the way I treated you. I would do anything to make what I did go away. I love you so much. I'm so miserable without you". He began to cry.
"Don't get upset. You'll be fine". I tried to stay calm and reassure him.
"I'm not strong like you. You are the strongest woman I have ever met. I need someone strong like you in my life. Do you miss me?" he asked.
"Yes", I replied. I did miss him.
"I knew you did. No one knows you like I do. No one in your whole life will love you the way I do. Do you still love me?"
Again I found myself replying" yes".
"Then let's meet. I really need to see you. I promise I won't hurt you. I'll never hurt you again.

Sour Face

I've got so much to tell you".
"I don't trust you". I didn't.
"Yes, I can understand why you don't trust me. I've treated you like shit, but I've changed. I love you and I know that you love me. We have this deep emotional bond you and I. We can't help the way we feel about each other. Please come out with me this week end." His voice was soft.
"I'm not sure". I was so confused. I just didn't know what to think.
"Please. I love you so much. Please come out with me. I really need to see you". He sounded so lost, so very sincere.
I found myself agreeing to see him that Saturday evening.

I was both nervous and excited at the thought of seeing him again. I was also worried about what my friends and family would say to me if they found out I was meeting him. I knew they would discourage me from seeing him. I didn't want to lose any of my friends; they had all been so supportive and loyal towards me. I felt that I was betraying them by agreeing to meet him. I was torn; did I do what I wanted to do, or what I should do? I wanted to see him again. I missed him. At that time I felt that I still loved him. This confused matters because my head told me that I shouldn't have any positive feelings towards someone who had been so cruel towards me .I felt that he was right I was mad, well not right in the head for feeling this way. My research has shown me I wasn't loosing the plot. I was a victim of traumatic

bonding.
I decided to keep the peace, and didn't tell anyone I was meeting him.

I took a very long time getting ready that evening. I looked at myself in the mirror. I was very pleased with the results of my efforts. I felt a very attractive as I put on my jacket and headed towards the taxi rank.
I had arranged to meet him in a bar we occasionally visited. Ten thousand butterflies' fluttered in my stomach as I paid the cab driver and walked into the building.
It was the early evening so the bar was fairly quiet. I scanned the room. There was no sign of him. I ordered a drink from the bar and sat at a table near to the door. I sat and waited for him.
He arrived ten minutes later. He had also taken a lot of time and effort with his appearance. He looked gorgeous.
He stood in the doorway of the bar, looking around the room. He smiled when he spotted me sitting at the table.
I stood up to meet him.
He greeted me with "You look absolutely stunning".
"Thanks. You look very smart", I replied.
He leaned in towards me. The fragrance of his pungent aftershave drifted up into my nostrils. The smell was so familiar. I found myself slipping back into the role of his "girl friend". He hugged me loosely, placing a kiss on my cheek at the same time.
"I'll go and get myself a drink. Do you want

anything?" he asked.

I didn't. No alcohol anyway. I wanted to keep a clear head.

I watched him as he walked across the room. I continued to stare at him as he stood at the bar.

"He's so attractive", my heart said, "you've forgotten how sexy and cute he is".

"Hang on", my head replied, "Remember how he treated you, like dirt most of the time. He's beaten you up and threatened to kill you. That's not a nice way to behave towards someone you're supposed to love".

"You knew he had some issues before you started the relationship. He was very drunk when he beat you up. He had been drinking all day remember", my heart replied. "He can be so nice to you when he wants to be, particularly when you don't annoy him"

He returned to the table before my head could reply, carrying two gin and tonics.

"It's your favourite brand of gin. I know you said you didn't want a drink, but I'd really like it if we could have a real drink together like we used to.

I took the glass from his outstretched hand.

He sat down opposite me, looking directly into my eyes.

"So how are you?" He asked me.

"I've not been very good at all. I haven't been sleeping much. I haven't been eating either. The thought of food makes me feel sick".

"You look like you've lost loads of weight. You look very skinny now." He said as he studied my figure. "I prefer you with more weight on your thighs and stomach".

"I haven't been on a diet or tried to lose weight on purpose. You know that I can't eat when I'm stressed". I was very defensive.

"Please just calm down, you look good. I noticed that several men were looking at you whilst I was at the bar".

I ignored his comments.

He changed the subject. "I'm moving out of that bed sit. It's a fucking shit hole. It's so fucking dirty. The place stinks. I've been in touch with a letting agency for professional people. I'm going to look at a flat over the weekend". He sipped his drink.

"I've made a couple of friends since we split up. Both of them are divorced men, who I met in the library. We've been out a few times. They are desperate to pull a woman. I don't think either of them has had a shag for a long time". He looked directly into my eyes. "I'm not interested in any woman. I want my woman, I want you back".

I quickly changed the subject.

"Have you spoken to any of your friends? Several of them have telephoned the house trying to contact you. They had left messages on your mobile phone."

"Yes I received all of the messages they left for me. I can't return their phone calls; in fact I can't be mates with any of them ever again. That's because they know what I did you to you. I can't go into that part of town, I'm concerned that some mad fucker will make it their duty to come and give me a good beating".

"No one is going to do that to you", I quickly reassured him. "You are over reacting. I know its difficult going to places where you may bump into

Sour Face

people we both knew. But I've done it. It gets easier after the first time".

"You can say that. People feel sorry for you because of what happened. They just hate me and think I'm a bastard".

I didn't reply. I began to sir my drink with the plastic stick, the ice cubes swirling around the bottom of the glass. He reached across the table and placed his hand on the top of the glass.

"Do you hate me, for what I did to you?" He asked me.

"No. I don't like you for what you did. But I don't hate you. It would be a lot easier for me if I did."

"Well I would hate me if I was you. I want you to know that I don't like what I did to you and if I could turn back the clock I would. We were happy before I got drunk and behaved like a prick. But what you have to remember is that I was fucking hammered. I had been drinking all day. I really didn't know what I was doing".

"You were happy", I replied." You had everything you wanted. Someone to wait on you hand and foot, cook your meals, do your washing and ironing. What did you do for me? I'll tell you what you did, picked fault with everything I did, bullied me constantly and spoke to me like I was a piece of rubbish".

"I know I treated you badly at times, but I really am sorry. I will change and I'm prepared to do anything to get you back. I'll even go and get professional help. I've got this for you to read".

He pulled a folded piece of paper from out of his pocket; placing it on the table he pushed it towards me.

"Open it", he instructed me. "It's information about domestic abuse for men who have hit their partners. I found the details of this organisation on the Internet. They do have a local branch. It's not government funded, so there is a cost. It is fucking expensive, but I don't care about the cost I will pay anything to have you back".

He reached across the table again and held my hand.

He continued the conversation. "How these sessions work is that I attend group therapy sessions and discuss my problems and why I get angry with you. The partners of the men involved also go. This means that everyone's point of view can be discussed openly".

I was horrified.

"Hang on a minute. It's you who needs help not me."

"Don't be so fucking negative", he snapped. "Other women will be there. This group is for couples, where one partner has been violent towards the other. They have decided to say together and are trying to get the relationship back on the right path".

"I can't do that. I don't trust you. If I went into a group and explained how you dragged me up the stairs by my hair, I would be convinced you would hit me when we got back home".

"That wouldn't happen", he tried to reassure me." I know you don't trust me, I understand why. But I really believe that in time you will learn to trust me again."

"I don't know if I do want to trust you again. What would my friends and family say if we got together

Sour Face

again? They would think that I was a real waste of space and never help me again." I spoke my thoughts aloud.

"This isn't about your fucking family and friends. You know how I hate other people interfering in our business." He looked at me. "This is about you and me. It's about what we both want. No one else matters. If I hadn't got drunk and hit you, we would still be together living our life".

He was right. I wouldn't have left him, even though I knew I couldn't continue to live my life that way, if he hadn't beaten me. I was so conditioned into believing that I couldn't function without him.

I just didn't know what to say.

"Forget the group therapy stuff for now. I don't want to freak you out. I just wanted you to know that I'm serious about getting help, proper help. I want to stop being a bastard to you."

"You need professional help. But you have to want to take the advice that's given ", I answered him.

"I think we should get relationship counselling. My mother agrees with me. If it's alright with you I'll make an appointment for us"

"Why on earth would I want to go there", I was amazed at his suggestion.

"We both know there are problems in the relationship. You have to take responsibility for your part in our problems. You have real issues that need to be dealt with. The main issue is with alcohol. You are a nasty cunt when you have been drinking", he said.

"What about you and the way you bully me?" I was beginning to get annoyed with him.

"Don't call me a fucking bully. I know what being bullied is all about, thanks to my fucking dad. I don't fucking bully you like he fucking bullied me. I'm not that fucking evil". He glared at me.

"Are you telling me that you are prepared to go into a room and discuss every detail of our relationship with a stranger, who will probably be a woman?"

"I'll do what I have to do to get you back. We can't go back to where we were in our relationship; I know that we have to move forward. I think we need professional help to do that. It's not all my fault. I'm not a complete bastard. I do get very angry but most of the time it's because you wind me up", he replied.

"If that is really true, why don't you lose your temper with other people? It's only me that you get mad with. It's only me you call abusive names. It's only me that you are physically aggressive towards. Other people upset you and you wait until you are alone with me. Then you will vent all that anger onto me. That shows me you have control over your anger. You choose to use your anger against me". I stared at him.

He returned my stare.

"Don't screech at me. You know I hate it".

"I'm not even raising my voice. What you don't like is that I'm answering you back. You are not right all of the time. That is a fact. I am not letting you treat me how you have done in the past. I'm not agreeing to all you say just to keep the peace."

"I don't want to fall out with you, or have a fucking row with you. I want us to try again. Make a fresh start. I'll wait as long as it takes for you to have me

Sour Face

back. I'll never love anyone the way I love you."
He leant forward in his seat.
"I still love you and I know that you still love me. All I am asking for is a chance. Please, give me a second chance. I want us to start going out again. I want to court you. I want to take you out on dates. I really miss you. Please I'm begging you".
His eyes were large and moist with tears. His voice shook with emotion.
"Don't get upset", I reassured him. "I can't be in a room on my own with you. I don't trust you. I will go out with you but only in public places. At the first sign of aggression of any kind, this includes verbal abuse, I will leave and you will never see me again".
"Thank you so much. You won't regret it. You have made me so happy. You know how good we are together. Let's go to that seventy's bar you like to celebrate.
He stood up, smiling broadly.
"I'd like that", I smiled back at him "we haven't been there for a very long time".
He helped me on with my jacket. He took my hand in his and we left the bar together.

In the weeks that followed I felt I was living a double life.
My nerves were on edge as I kept the relationship secret from both my family and friends.
Each time anyone asked me to go out with them; I would make an excuse, and go and spend time with him.
Why on earth would I do that? Why would I risk losing my family and friends by spending time with

someone who had treated me so badly?

At the time, I really thought I was going mad.

My head was telling me that what I was doing was wrong; giving me a list of reasons why I shouldn't be seeing him again. The main reason was how unsafe I was due to his unprovoked aggression.

Whatever my head said, my heart always had a logical answer.

One of my principles in life is that everyone deserves a second chance.

I believed with all my heart that he did.

I still believed that he wasn't responsible for the way he had treated me in the past. I made the excuse that he was drunk, so was unaware of what he was doing when he beat me.

Research from an article by David Hansen written in 2007 states" alcohol doesn't and can't make one person abuse another. Men use alcohol as an excuse for violence. They attempt to rid themselves of responsibility for the problem by blaming it on the effects of the alcohol".

Other articles I have read on the subject of alcohol and domestic violence agree with Hansen. They clearly state that alcohol is not the cause of domestic violence.

I also still took responsibility for the last physical attack, believing that if I hadn't answered him back he wouldn't have hit me.

My head didn't trust him, not one bit. I also didn't believe that he would never hurt me again. In that part of me, the part I call my "knower", I knew he would still hurt me, yet I still gave him a second chance. I was convinced that I could continue to manage his behaviour and that I was the person in control of the situation.

I was very wrong. There was only one person in control of our relationship. That situation would never change. He would always be in control of every aspect of our relationship and indeed my life, for as long as we remained together.

His behaviour towards me over those first weeks of our new courtship was faultless. He used my real name at all times. He told me I was beautiful. He arranged for us to have dinner at a new stylish restaurant, picking me up from work to surprise me. Every day he would ask me to live with him again. I repeatedly replied no. I told him I wasn't ready. The real reason was that I didn't trust him.

As the weeks went past I found myself feeling more at ease with him, until I reached the point where I felt comfortable about being alone with him. In fact I wanted to be alone with him. I wanted to know if his behaviour had really changed as he claimed. There was only one way to find if his promises were true; that was to be alone in a room with him.

He asked me to visit him at his new flat.

"Let's have a quiet night in", he suggested. "This going out four times a week is wearing me out and also doing damage to my bank account".

"Why don't you come to the house? I'll cook something for us", I replied. I thought I would be in control if he came to the house, as he would be on my territory.

"I can't go back to that fucking house. It holds too many bad memories for me. I was arrested there twice remember".

I ignored his remarks.

"Well, I'll have to come to you then. I'll cook a meal at home and bring the food with me".

He smiled at me. "That's great. I've really missed your cooking. I'll get a bottle of that French red wine you really like".

"It's OK. I'm not that bothered about drinking, particularly during the week". I was back in my coping mode already. I knew he didn't like me drinking any alcohol. I didn't want to upset him in any way.

"I want to buy it for you. Please let me. It'll be really nice to have a quality bottle of wine with a decent home cooked meal. It'll be like the good times we used to have".

I agreed to him buying the wine and arranged to meet him at his flat the following evening.

I arrived at his flat at 7pm, accompanied by his favourite homemade foods.

He lived in a quiet residential area of town. The flat he lived in was located on the ground floor of a three story Victorian house, which had been converted into four flats.

He answered the door- bell with a warm smile, hugging me as I stood in the doorway.

He ushered me along the hallway to his flat, where he took my coat and hung it on the hooks situated on the wall.

Piles of un- ironed clothes were placed in rows along the small hallway, together with several black plastic dustbin bags stuffed full of various items.

I had to squeeze past these obstacles in order to reach the sitting room.

Sour Face

He opened the door at the end of the hall -way, and invited me into the sitting room.

Newspapers and magazines were scattered across the floor and covered the small coffee table in the centre of the room.

Every piece of furniture was draped with items of his clothing. I could see various items of foot ware, tossed underneath the television cabinet.

I was amazed at the untidiness of this room. He wouldn't have tolerated the same mess in the house we shared.

He noticed me looking around the room

"I know. It's a fucking tip. What you have to remember is that I don't do anything domestic. I don't care about how I live; it really doesn't matter to me. The only thing that matters is you and me getting back together permanently

I quickly changed the subject and walked towards the hallway.

"Where's your kitchen and I'll warm up the food?"

He gestured to the door on my left.

I found the kitchen in the same disarray as the rest of the flat.

He went back into the sitting room and left me to organize the food.

I had to clear a space on the work- top in order to serve the food I had brought with me.

I carried the food together with all the equipment we needed to eat it with back into the sitting room.

He had moved some of the clothes making a space for us to sit on the sofa.

After we had finished eating he handed me his plate and I found myself taking it along with all of the other equipment we had used back into the kitchen.

Fifteen minutes later I had washed all of the dirty crockery that had filled the sink and spilt on to the surrounding work- tops. I felt I had to. How could I just wash up the various pots that had contained the food I had brought? I felt that would have been selfish of me.

I then dried all of the various pots and pans, put them away and bleached all of the worktops and sink. I was sweeping the floor when he appeared at the kitchen door.

"What are you doing? I didn't ask you to clear up after me". He looked at me. "I knew you would though. I'm grateful you did the washing up. I was running out of mugs."

We went back into the sitting room together.

The soft glow of lamp- light now filled the room, soft music played in the background.

"If I didn't know any better I would think that you were trying to seduce me", I tried to make a joke the situation.

"That's the general idea". His face told me he was being deadly serious. "I've missed you, physically missed you. I like regular sex, that's what being in a relationship is all about. I've also missed your cooking. You are an excellent cook; in fact you are the best cook I have ever been out with".

"Well it makes a change to be told that I'm good at something. Usually your telling me how rubbish I am, that I can't do anything right".

"There's no need to be fucking sarcastic. I hate it when you talk to me like I'm a cunt. There's no need to treat me like an idiot".

I found myself apologising for my behaviour.

Sour Face

"That's OK. Let's get back to our original conversation. Yes I am trying to seduce you. Have you got tights on underneath your jeans?" He asked.

"No I don't wear them anymore. They make me feel too hot", I replied.

He looked at me in disbelief.

"I asked you here on our first date alone and you don't ware any fucking tights!" He began to shout at me.

"Don't raise your voice at me. I've told you I'm not putting up with your behaviour anymore. I didn't want to wear tights so I didn't. This is the way it's going to be from now on. I'm not letting you dictate to me ever again".

I said the words as firmly as I could, whilst quickly scanning the room, looking at how far away I was from the door.

"I'm sick of telling you, not to fucking answer me back, sour face bitch".

He got up from the sofa and stood in front of me.

I began to panic.

"It's time for me to leave. I'll get my coat".

Grabbing my handbag I stood up and walked around him, heading towards the door.

"Why are you leaving?" He asked.

"I have told you that I am not accepting any type of aggression from you any more".

"Is this what is going to happen every time you disagree with me, you are just going to run away? Fucking sour face cunt"

"Yes, I will always leave if you talk to me in that manner. I hate that word and you know I do. That's why you use it. No one I know gets called that terrible word every day. It's not right and I won't tolerate it anymore."

"It's obvious this relationship isn't going to work", he glared at me. "I can't be with someone where I'm not allowed to be myself. Where I have to watch what I say or how I behave in case I fuck them off. I can't live my life with threats of you leaving me at any opportunity hanging over my head".

"Well that's exactly how I have lived my life over the past two years, watching what I say, what I wear and how I behave in case I upset you".

"Stop being a cunt", he replied." You haven't changed at all. You are always the fucking same when you've had a drink".

"I've had one glass of wine. That doesn't make me drunk or an alcoholic with drink issues. You just don't want me to answer you back. You want to be in complete control and I'm not letting you do that anymore".

"Look I'm sorry. Please stay. You know what I'm like. I won't allow myself to be dictated to by a fucking woman. So answer me, why do you try and call all the shots? Are you deliberately trying to wind me up?"

"No, I'm not. All I expect from you is to be treated like a human being, with respect. That includes no name- calling, particularly being called the horrible "C" word. I don't see that as me being a dictator. I want to be treated as other women are in loving relationships."

"You've become too fucking opinionated. I am me. I'll do what I want, when I want and if you don't like it you know where the fucking door is".

Sour Face

"Yes I do. That's what I'm going to do right now".

I turned away from him to open the door, placing my hand on the door handle.

He pulled my hand from the door handle. Then placing both of his hands on my shoulders he spun me around and pushed me against the wall. Gripping my arms with both hands he kept me pinned there, standing directly in front of me.

I began to cry. I knew what was going to happen next.

"Shut up; fucking sour face cunt, the fucking neighbours will hear you".

"Let me go. All I want to do is go home".

"Fucking shut up. I don't give a fuck about what you want. Stop fucking answering me back, you're winding me up on purpose".

He let go of me and took a step backwards out of my personal space.

I moved away from the wall.

A split second later, he grabbed my neck and mouth with his hands. He then jarred my neck backwards and then let go of me.

I lost my balance and fell onto the floor, my head knocking against the wall as I fell.

I slowly got up from the floor. My lip was bleeding badly.

He stood in the doorway watching me.

"It's your own fucking fault. You shouldn't have wound me up. You just don't know when to fucking shut up".

I ignored him, trying to compose myself. I picked up my bag from the floor and walked towards the door.

"I'm leaving now", I said looking directly at him. "If

you won't let me pass I will scream as loud as I can to get the neighbours attention".

"You fucking would do as well", he snarled at me. "I'm not preventing you from leaving. In fact I want you to fuck off", he shouted, stepping away from the door.

I walked down the hallway as quickly as I could. My hands were shaking as I fumbled with the lock on the front door. Finally opening it, I stepped outside slamming it firmly shut behind me.

CHAPTER THIRTEEN

The phone calls began as soon as I arrived home. I turned off my mobile.

The shrill sound of ringing from the landline filled the hallway and drifted past me into the upper part of the house.

I sat on the bottom step of the staircase staring at the telephone.

"How could you have been so stupid?" my head asked me.

"You've allowed him to do what you promised your self would never happen to you again. You have let him physically hurt you".

I got up from the step and examined my face in the mirror.

My bottom lip was swollen a cut was visible stretching the depth of my lip. As a result of my crying smudges of makeup appeared underneath my eyes. My hair was untidy and ruffled. I looked a mess.

"Look at yourself", my head continued." Look at the state you're in. This is all because you allowed him back into your life. Why did you do it?" I felt so ashamed.

"You did this because you are a decent human being. You felt that he deserved a second chance. You wanted to do the right thing. You wanted to prove to yourself and to him that you have been fair towards him, that you didn't just dismiss him when things got tough as other women have done in the past," my heart replied." You can look yourself in the eye and honestly say that you've given this relationship your very best shot".

"But why did you expose yourself to such danger?" my head asked in despair. "You knew in the deepest part of your knower that he would hurt you again. All of the people who care about you told you this would happen if you got involved with him again. They were right. You knew they were. Why can't you just let go of him? You know that he is no good for you. Why have you still got feelings for him when he has treated you so very badly? You must be going mad, he was right you have got a screw loose".

Of course I now know that I was not going mad. I had been so conditioned. I was a victim of traumatic bonding and battered woman's syndrome. I hadn't heard of any of these theories back then. I wish I had done, I wouldn't have felt so stupid, defeated and dim.

"You still think that you can change him", my head continued. "He's never going to change because he doesn't want to".

The hallway was now silent. I continued to look at my reflection in the hall mirror. "You can't see him anymore. You have to end this relationship for good. I don't know how you are going to do this but you have to find a way. His violence towards you is going to increase. The fact he's on a bind over order doesn't matter to him. He'll never stop hurting you because he knows that you will take responsibility for his behaviour. You need to face up to the fact that he wants to hurt you and will always find excuses for doing so."

The silence was pierced by the shrill tone of the telephone ringing from the land-line.

I reached for the telephone. Unplugging it from the

Sour Face

socket, I turned off the light in the hallway and went slowly up the stairs to bed.

The next morning I plugged the phone back into the wall socket. Instantly it rang.
I allowed the phone to be answered.
His voice filled the hallway.
"Why are you being such a fucking bitch? I know you've turned the phone off because the answering machine wasn't picking up my calls. Why aren't you speaking to me? You are winding me up on purpose. You know that I won't be fucking ignored. Why won't you answer me? You can't have gone to work this fucking early." His voice gradually grew louder until he was shouting into the phone. "You fucking cunt. I can't believe you have resorted to your old trick of running away like a thief in the night again. I fucking hate you". He hung up.
I stood there in the hallway watching the flickering orange light of the answering machine. I pressed the button on the machine and deleted the message.
"You can't go on like this; turning the phone off every time you want peace", my head told me. "You must change your number".
"But then he wouldn't be able to get in touch with you", my heart replied. "He needs you and you need him. How are you both going to cope on your own?"
"You'll survive", my head replied. "You know it's going to be hard, but you'll work out a way to cope. The first thing you must do is change the landline number. There is no time like the present.

Do it now".

I rang the telephone company and explained that I wanted to change my telephone number.

The sales assistant asked me the reasons for this and I briefly explained the situation stressing the fact I was receiving unwanted phone calls from my ex partner.

She reassured me that the number could be changed quickly and would be free of charge. At my request she would also arrange for my new number to be ex directory. A few minutes later she gave me my new telephone number and told me it would be in service within twenty- four hours. That was all I needed to do.

I felt a mixture of relief and sadness as I replaced the handset of the land- line. I quickly dismissed the feelings of sadness.

"OK. What you need to do now is change the number of your mobile". My head was talking again.

"But there's a problem in doing that. The company won't let you change the number because the contract is in his name not yours," my heart answered.

"If you can't change the number then you will have to change the phone", my head replied. "What are you doing with that old type of mobile phone? You know the reason why. It's because he was stuck in a contract and wanted the latest model so he decided that you could have his old phone and he would have an all singing and dancing new one."

It was true. I found his phone difficult to use and the tariff very expensive.

He would scold me when I complained.

Sour Face

"I wish you would stop fucking moaning. You should be glad you've got a fucking contract phone. Most people would be glad they have a contract phone, but then you're not like most fucking people, you are a fucking stuck up sour face bitch".

My head was talking again.

"You owe him nothing. It's his phone therefore his responsibility to pay the bill. You don't have to keep the phone out of misplaced loyalty to him. You need a phone of your own".

I didn't know how to go about obtaining a contract mobile phone, but my head convinced me to find out.

After work the same day I found myself in a mobile phone shop.

I was very honest with the sales assistant and explained that I knew nothing at all about mobile phones. I did know how much I wanted to pay each month and that I wanted to be able to use the phone easily.

The young sales assistant told me I reminded him of his mother (she didn't have a clue about mobiles either) and went out of his way to be helpful.

Within the space of twenty- four hours I had changed both of my personal contact numbers. He had no way of contacting me by telephone. He did how ever have my works telephone number there was nothing I could do about that. If he wanted to telephone me at work I wouldn't be able to stop him. However my work place did employ full time receptionists. These staff members answered the telephones during office hours. They answered and screened most of my calls before putting them through to my extension. They would ask for the identity of each caller. This process would make contacting me not impossible but rather difficult for him.

I wrote down a list of everything physical he had ever done to me.
I followed this with a list of every name he had ever called me; every time he had undermined me during the last six months of the relationship and every detail of his ritualistic cleaning schedule.
It took a very long time to complete these lists, as they were extensive.
Once they were complete I read through the several sheets of paper.
"Right", my head told me, "the next time you think about starting a relationship with him, read these lists. Stop making excuses for his behaviour, concentrate on the facts. You don't want to be with a man who treats you in this appalling way. You want to be happy. Being with him makes you miserable. Every time your heart tells you that you love him, or have feelings for him, get these lists out. As you read them remember each event and how you felt as he abused you. That will help to suppress those feelings. You have to put those feelings away lock them in a box and keep them there until you can eventually throw the box away. You have to end and survive this relationship. This is your way to do it."
So I began using this coping strategy. The next time I spoke to him it was fully implemented.

Sour Face

Why hadn't I reported the incident to the police?

He was on a bind over order to keep the peace towards me. He'd broken that court order by being physically abusive towards me. The cut lip I had received was physical evidence of his abuse.

The answer to this question was fear.

Fear of what my family and friends would say when they found out I'd been seeing him without telling anyone. I was worried that no one would want to know me when they knew what I'd been doing. I felt that I had let them all down badly.

I was also afraid of being ridiculed by the police if I reported the incident. I had pressed charges against him twice. He received two separate punishments for his crimes against me.

Yet I had still gone to see him alone, I'd begun a courtship with him. I had become one of those victims the police had told me about. The one's who wasted their time by returning to the abuser after the court case was complete.

Memories of what had happened previously at court filled my head .No one had believed me when I told them he had threatened to kill me. The reason for that was because I had gone to see him alone that day outside the bank.

I was convinced that officials would think that what happened to me was my own fault. I had gone to see him on my own I had deserved what had happened to me.

I couldn't face the whole procedure again, particularly as I would have to deal with everything alone.

So I made the decision I couldn't report this incident. I would tell him the relationship was definitely over.

The more I said those words; the more I tried to convince myself they were true.

My head kept on imploring me to listen.

"It's over because of his violent behaviour towards you. Remember he will never change. Focus on the bad times".

I was still worried about how he was going to cope without me.

I was looking for my passport. It wasn't in the usual place. I unsuccessfully searched various drawers in my bedroom. I widened my search. I decided to check the various boxes and files that lived in the spare bedroom.

The second box I opened contained various envelopes. I noticed the corner of my passport wallet sticking out amongst them. I picked up the heavy box and balanced it on the arm of the sofa. As I grabbed the leather cover of my passport the box tipped over. Its contents spilt across the floor.

Cursing my own clumsiness I stood the box upright and began the process of replacing all of the items as quickly as possible.

Across the floor were various photographs of Matt and Bernie as young children. I sat on the floor and spent a few minutes going through the pile of pictures; turning each one over and replacing the photographs in the box. I smiled fondly at each one.

I turned over the next picture. It was a picture of me taken on holiday the previous year. I studied the photograph. I was smiling, in fact I looked fairly attractive, but my eyes told the real story of my

Sour Face

situation.

They appeared full of pain. There was no warmth shinning out of them. I place the picture in the pile of rubbish I had created.

I turned over more photographs then gasped in surprise. His smiling face looked back at me. I was convinced that I had thrown every picture of him and us as a couple away.

I began to cry. I was trying so hard to forget him, to concentrate on the negative aspects of the relationship.

The pictures brought back memories of when I thought I was happy, when I believed there was a reason for his behaviour. You think that you've got everything under control; you are in the frame of mind to deal with him. I kept concentrating on his negative behaviour towards me. I told myself that I had put him in a box with the lid on. That was the job completed I could now get on with life.

Then a song comes on the radio, or you find a picture or an old birthday card and your resolve goes on holiday. You become a crumpled emotional wreck. The will of iron becomes one made of butter that just melts.

"Stop crying ", my head shouted at me. "You weren't happy. Can you remember a full month when he never abused you in any way? You can't remember because there was never such a time. He treated you like dirt. Stop crying. You've wasted enough time crying over him".

I gathered the pictures of him together, tearing each one in half. I then went outside and threw all of the pieces into the black plastic dustbin. Replacing the dustbin lid with force I returned into the house and to the job of sorting out the items that remained on the bedroom floor.

It is natural to feel upset. I had to grieve; in fact it was important for me to grieve. Not for the end of the relationship, but for me. I had to realise that I was a victim, or rather had been a victim of domestic abuse. It was very difficult to come to terms with the fact that I was a victim. This was because for a long time I still took the responsibility for his behaviour towards me. It was only when I began to research the subject of domestic abuse and the relevant theories that I finally realised none of what happen to me was my fault.

I had been a victim I wanted to be a survivor.

My office telephone continuously rang. I ran and answered it out of breath.

"Why won't you fucking answer my calls?" He demanded.

"I have nothing further to say to you", I replied.

"Why are you being so fucking hostile towards me? I haven't done anything wrong to you".

"I'm not being hostile; all I'm being is honest. I told you from the start, any sign of aggression towards me would result in the end of the relationship. I'm not putting up with anymore of your abusive behaviour". I made my voice sound firm and controlled. Inside I was screaming.

"Fucking listen to you, miss self righteous sour face bitch. Who do you think you're fucking talking to? I just want to know one thing."

"I'm not talking to you any more", I replied. "I'm ending this conversation now".

Sour Face

"Wait. Please don't go. I'm sorry; I want to ask you a question. It's really important that you give me a truthful answer. I'll then hang up once you've answered, I promise."

"I'm listening now. I'll stop listening if you start shouting and swearing at me. I've told you that I'm not prepared to put up with your abusive behaviour."

"Ok, I've stopped being stupid. Have you contacted the police about the argument we had at my flat?" He asked.

"No I haven't, and we didn't have an argument". That was the reason he was ringing me. He was worried about being arrested.

"Why haven't you contacted them?"

"I have my reasons for not contacting them. Before you ask me I'm not telling you. There's no need to worry you won't be arrested".

"I don't fucking believe you, or fucking trust you after what you did last time "

"It's not my problem if you don't believe me. I'm telling you the truth. I have not involved the police".

"I know the reason why you haven't contacted the fucking police, you still love me", he declared.

"No I don't", I was now alarmed, the last thing I wanted was for him to get the idea in his head that we would get back together again.

"I don't believe you again. Any other woman would have grassed me up to the filth. The only reason you haven't done that is because you still love me. You can't convince me otherwise; you still love me. That thought gives me hope. I know that we will get back together and live as a proper couple."

Before I could object he hung up.

The following day I received another phone call at work.

"Please stop harassing me at work", I asked him.

"I can't talk to you any other way. The fucking phone at the house isn't working".

"The phone is working fine. I've changed the phone number. I don't want you constantly ringing me".

"Why have you done that?" He demanded.

"I've told you why. I can't talk to you anymore. This relationship is over"

"It's only fucking over when I say it is. I know that you are still in love with me", he answered.

"I'm not in love with you, why won't you believe me", I asked trying so hard not to shout at him. "I just want you to leave me alone".

"I'm not doing anything wrong. I'm just talking to a woman who is in love with me and who keeps on encouraging me to telephone her. I am ringing to sort out our finances. I want twenty thousand pounds out of that house. I want you to sell it and move out. My friends at work think it's disgusting how you haven't made me a decent offer. It's my house as well; my name is on that deed. I don't fucking care about how fair the situation is, or that you put all of the deposit. I just want my money".

"I've told you before, anything financial needs to go through solicitors. You need to appoint one and they will sort out all of the paper work. You don't need to speak to me at all".

He ignored my last remark.

"I've made an appointment to see a counsellor. I

Sour Face

want you to come with me. I can't do it on my own".

I was amazed. "I'm not going any where with you. When will you realise I'm not your emotional crutch. You need to get your mother to support you".

"I don't want any help from my fucking mother. All I'm asking you for is a little bit of support. You owe me that. All this fucking mess is your fault for involving the police"

"I'm not prepared to go any where with you. This relationship is over. I can't go back to the way things were between us".

"I don't want you back. It was never going to work. You wouldn't even tell your fucking friends and family we were seeing each other. You hid me away like a bad smell. That's no way to treat anybody. You were ashamed of me".

All of what he said was true. I wouldn't go any where with him where I thought anyone I knew would be. I didn't want any one to know about him and me. I was very ashamed of myself; for being so weak and stupid.

"I just want to know that you are there in the background if I need you", he continued, "I don't want to be with you. The relationship was completely wrong for me".

"I'm not waiting in the wings for you to call me every time you have a crisis. I'm not your counsellor or your nurse".

"You are a fucking nasty unhelpful cunt. I'll fucking kill you", he screamed the words down the phone as he hung up.

Two minutes later he rang me back.

"I'm not really going to kill you. You just made me angry. You haven't contacted the police have you?" He sounded concerned.

"No I haven't. You can't keep ringing me at work I'm busy". I replied.

"You should have thought about that before you changed your personal phone numbers. Any way I don't want to talk to you any more. You fucking bore me to death". He hung up.

That evening the doorbell at home rang. Thinking it was Bernie who usually forgot her key I answered the door, opening it wide.

"You'd forget your head if it wasn't attached ", I said. There was no answer. I looked up.

He stood outside the front door

A mixture of fear and surprise ran through my body.

"What are you doing here"? I asked him.

"I've come to see you. This is half my house and I can come here when I want to. There is nothing you can do to stop me", he said defiantly.

As soon as he finished talking he pushed me out of the doorway and strode into the house.

He stood in the hallway.

I was petrified.

"I want you to leave ", I said as firmly as I could. I remained standing in the doorway my body propping open the front door.

"I'm not going fucking anywhere. I want to talk to you. Come away from the door and let's chat".

"No I'm not going to do what you want. If you won't leave I'm going to call the police".

Sour Face

"I have every right to be here. You seem to have conveniently forgotten that I own half of this house. Ring the fucking police. They won't do any thing. We've been seeing each other. You have encouraged me. You haven't got a leg to stand on ", he gloated.

"That's a risk I'm prepared to take. What you forget is that you are on a bind over order to keep the peace towards me. I haven't invited you here tonight. You have forced your way into the house. I have told you several times that this relationship is over."

"Fucking bitch", he yelled as he took several steps towards me.

"If you come any closer I'll scream. I want you to leave now", I shouted.

People passing the house were looking across the drive at the two of us through the open front door.

I reached for my mobile phone that was in its usual place, in the pocket of my jeans.

"I'm fucking going anyway. There is no need to be so fucking nasty. You are always fucking over reacting".

He stepped towards me. I squeezed my body against the front door making the space in the doorway as large as possible.

He walked through the doorway and out onto the drive without saying a word.

As soon as he was out of the house I slammed and bolted the front door shut.

I stood with my back against the door, crying softly at first then increasing until my whole body was shaking with the intensity of my sobs.

The next morning I rang the domestic violence unit at my local police station.

I explained fully to the female officer the events of the past few weeks and the details of the previous night.

The officer I spoke to was professional and supportive, not at all judgemental as I was expecting her to be.

The police officer told me I had to make sure that I made my feelings to him known. In order to do this I had to be very blunt and use simple words that he wouldn't misunderstand or manipulate.

Once I had done that I had to make sure that I contacted the police if he made any further contact with me.

After I had finished speaking to the police officer I decided to write down what I was going to say to him when he next contacted me.

I would make the statement short. I wanted to make my point before he would interrupt me as he usually did.

Having a written statement would also prove to the police what I had actually said to him.

He rang me at work two days later.

"I want to speak to you", I said to him my voice shaking with emotion.

"That's good because I want to fucking talk to you as well" he replied.

"This relationship is over. I don't want to talk to you again, I don't want you to ring me at work or visit the house. If you contact me again I'll ring the police and you will be arrested for breaking the bind over order".

"Fuck you", he replied.

Sour Face

"I mean what I say. If you break the conditions of your bind over order by contacting me I'll contact the police and you will be arrested". I put the phone down before he could reply.

Over the following weeks we began to experience nuisance telephone calls at work. The phone calls all followed the same pattern. The person would hang up as soon as one of my colleagues said hello. Following my last conversation with him I deliberately didn't answer the telephone at work.

My colleagues agreed to share this duty between them, after the receptionist had left for the day.

I felt guilty about this. I was worried that this would indicate that I wasn't doing my job properly.

My work colleagues reassured me that this wasn't the case.

The situation came to a head when my colleague had to answer the phone during a potential emergency situation as the phone was continuously ringing.

When she answered it the caller hung up.

She reported the situation to me. I just knew that it was him making those phone calls. He was trying to contact me.

I then decided to contact the telephone company, who referred me to the nuisance bureau. The advice and service they offered was excellent.

They advised us to log every call making a note of the exact time each call was made. Every morning I rang them with the times of these calls.

At the end of five days the telephone company contacted me. They had traced the telephone number of the nuisance calls. The calls were being made from a mobile telephone. That was the only information they were able to give me, as the data protection act prevented them from giving me any further details.

They advised me to contact the police as the telephone company could pass the information on to them.

I telephoned the police and two uniformed policemen came to work to see me.

I explained fully what had happened regarding my relationship, the bind over order and the recent phone calls.

I relayed the information the telephone company had given me, that they knew the identity of the nuisance caller. I went on to say that the telephone company required the police officers to complete a form and return it to the telephone company. The telephone company would then release the identity of the caller to them.

The police officers received guidance from the police station sergeant. They were very reluctant to complete the requested paper work, as it would be very time consuming. They were also concerned that the evidence against him wouldn't be "air- tight". This was because the phone calls were being made from a mobile. The accused person could claim that the phone had been stolen and that anyone could have made the calls.

The police officer suggested going to his flat to warn him. They would ask him if he was making the calls. If he admitted making the calls they would ask him to stop telephoning me.

I was flabbergasted.

"He'll deny it's him and increase the amount of

Sour Face

calls he makes. What about this bind over order? I thought he had to keep the peace towards me?" I asked.

The police officer explained that they would have to caution him first. If he continued to contact me after the caution then he would be arrested and taken back to court.

"I don't want you to speak to him. You'll just make the entire situation worse. I am amazed that you can't really help me".

The police officers explained again the reasons why they couldn't complete the extensive paper work and left my work place.

I felt so alone and defeated.

In the weeks that followed it felt like an uneasy truce had descended on me.

There were no further telephone calls to my work place.

Everything appeared to have returned to normal.

Bernie came to visit me.

"I don't want to alarm you mum, but I'm sure I've just seen his car parked opposite the drive".

We looked out of the sitting room window. There was no sign of him or his car.

The next day whilst I was opening my bedroom curtains I saw him drive past the house.

This continued over the next few days.

I changed the times I started and finished work. I didn't want him to know my routine.

A week later the phone calls at work began again.

I answered the telephone one afternoon. It was him.

"I just want you to know that I'm ringing about the

house. I want my money". He demanded.

"I'm not telling you anymore. You need to contact a solicitor", I replied.

"I'm not prepared to pay for a fucking solicitor. I can't afford it".

"Neither can I ", I replied.

"Can't we just sort out the details by ourselves"? He asked.

"No. That wouldn't work. You would try to manipulate me; make me do what you want".

"I would never do to that," he answered.

"I'm not arguing with you. That is all I have to say to you". My voice was firm.

"I'm lonely without you. I miss you. I know you don't fucking miss me. I know you are still going out. I saw you in the high street the other evening. Hasn't took you long to start looking for someone else", he sneered.

"If you are following me you had better stop doing so now. If I see you any where I am then I will contact the police".

He ignored me.

"Do you still love me? I love you and miss you."

"I don't love you," I answered.

"I don't believe you. You can't turn feelings off like a light switch. You and I have a deep bond that will always be there no matter where we are or who we're with".

"I don't love you and that's the truth. I don't want you to contact me again. If you do I will contact the police and that's a promise", I replied.

"Listen to you miss fucking prim. I want you to believe this. I swear on my mother's life that I have never fucking loved you", he screamed as he slammed the phone down.

A year later I answered the telephone at work.
His voice filled my ears. I felt physically sick.
"I need to settle the house with you. I've decided it's time to end this relationship. I don't want to go to solicitors we can agree on a figure right now. I want five thousand pounds. Everyone I've spoken to thinks I'm being extremely fair with you. Do you agree?" He asked me.
"I'm too shocked to agree to anything. I can't believe that I'm speaking to you" I replied.
"Well there's nothing to be shocked about. I'm just having a normal conversation with you. There's a lot of water gone under the bridge since we last spoke. I have moved on. Of course I wish you well for the future as I'm sure you would wish me the same".
I didn't respond. "So what do you think about that figure? I will not change my mind I will be really stubborn about it. I don't care that I was only in the house six months and that it was all of your money that was invested. The law states I'm entitled to half of that equity. You are getting a very good deal".
His arrogance angered me. "No I'm not. It's completely unfair and immoral. But I know I have no choice. I will have to give you that money. Appoint a solicitor and I'll start the process of getting you off the mortgage"
"That's agreed. Five thousand pounds and I'll sign the house over to you. I presume this will be the last time I speak to you?" He asked.
"Yes, there is no need for me to ever speak to you

again. I just want you out of my life for ever" I replied and placed the phone firmly back on the receiver.

Sour Face

CHAPTER FOURTEEN

At the beginning of our relationship he brought me a soft toy. A really pretty grey coloured fur cat with a pink ribbon collar. It was expensive, a good quality toy. It lived on my wooden blanket chest that I kept in my bedroom. When we separated I couldn't bear to look at it, as it reminded me of when he gave it to me, when I thought I was happy. I put it the corner of my spare room.

I decided to give it away, along with a few other items to a local charity shop. I decided that the Cat would need washing, as it was rather dusty. As I waited for the toy to finish washing, I watched as the Cat spun around the drum, slowly. Each time it stopped, the face of the Cat was always visible; it's eyes appearing to be looking straight at me. I became upset.

In that split second I was reminded of my past life. The Cat was a metaphor, of me going round and round trapped in a situation that I couldn't get out of. No one could open the door and get me out. No one came to rescue me, because I never asked for anyone's help.

I told people how happy I was; I talked about him and our life together in a very positive way. I was building this fantasy of two people who really cared about each other. I was kidding myself, desperately trying to reassure myself that we were all right as a couple. Of course we weren't, I was his victim.

I took the Cat from the washing machine and sat it on the radiator to dry.

I cried so much that night, almost ten months after

I had left him. I cried for myself, for how he had treated me. Each tear was a release of emotion, despair and unhappiness. I needed to let go of those feelings. I needed to mourn for me, for the loss of the person who disappeared for two years, locked away emotionally by him. I needed to put down that baggage and continue taking the small steps from survival to recovery.

The image of the toy Cat stayed with me for a few days.

The first evening back in my house was very strange. At six thirty I looked at the front door waiting to hear his key in the lock.

I sat in the living room .The silence overwhelmed me.

There was no one telling me what to cook, what to eat and when to go to bed. I had gone from someone giving me constant orders to nothing. I was never allowed time on my own, quality time to relax and pursue my hobbies. I was lost; I didn't know what to do.

When you leave the perpetrator, society thinks the story ends. He was violent to you, so you leave him; you are safe and can now live happily ever after. There is no fairy tale ending for victims of domestic violence. The end of the relationship is just the beginning of a long and difficult journey the victim has to make. It's good that the violence and verbal abuse has stopped no one wants to endure that. But what you are left with is so difficult to deal with, because you are in fact left with nothing. The whole of your life stretches out in front of you like an empty page.

Sour Face

Bedtime during those first few weeks I lived alone was very difficult. As he had attacked me in the bedroom we shared I found the room terrifying. I brought several sets of new bedding, pillows and a quilt. I threw all the bed linen we had slept on together away.

Before I went up to bed I would check all of the downstairs windows, and the back and front doors, several times to ensure that they were locked. I would also bolt all of the doors and remove the keys from the locks. I was convinced he was going to break in and hurt me.

I carried my mobile phone around with me, constantly, wherever I went in the house. At night-time I would carry it in my dressing gown pocket. I slept with it under my pillow. When I lived with him I used to sleep on the left hand side of the bed facing the wall. I developed a pattern of sleeping facing the bedroom door so I would be able to see him coming up the stairs if he broke into my house.

I found myself unable to settle in the sitting room as I felt he could watch me easily from outside of the window.

I sat for long periods in the spare room. I felt safe there, the only room he'd never physically attacked me in.

I slept several weeks on the sofa in there, curled up with my mobile in a sleeping bag.

Weekends were lonely, two days ahead to spend by myself.

I developed a schedule, a timetable, of tasks and jobs to do. It would start from the time I got up until the time I went to bed. Each hour of the day had an allocated job. These varied from doing my washing and ironing to going shopping. As I had forgotten how to spend my relaxing time, I also developed a schedule for each evening. This involved such activities as reading, watching television for a certain length of time or weeding the garden. I would ask friends round once in the week and would cook for them. Bernie and Matt invited themselves twice a week and we would go out for a cheap and cheerful meal or have a take away.

As the months past, I found that I didn't need this ritualistic schedule to get through the days. I had learnt how to be on my own again. I began to enjoy the freedom of doing what I wanted. If I didn't fancy cooking then I wouldn't. If I wanted to meet with a friend straight after work then I did.

I remained conditioned for a long time. I would still clean the house to the regime that had been imposed on me. I would still take off the cooker knobs and clean under them. I would still bleach the sink and clean behind the back of the taps. I would scrub the showerhead with a soap pad until the stainless steel shone.

I employed a man to mow the grass and help keep the gardens tidy.

My brain was telling me to keep the house clean and tidy at all times, maintain his standards because he may come and check the house today. If he can't inspect the place today, he may send his mother round instead. The house must be spotless just in case that happened; I didn't want him thinking that I couldn't look after the house by myself.

Sour Face

These were illogical thought patterns, but my brain was in overload. It had to learn to function again. I had to re learn how to think for myself.

I also had to re-educate myself regarding my financial situation. I was scared about managing my money. I had forgotten how to budget and control my outgoings.
I panicked at the thought of being over drawn. As hard as I tried I couldn't dismiss his words of constant criticism that filled my head.
"You are fucking useless with money. You spend it like water; you will never be able to manage financially on your own".
He had taken complete control of my money.
So I developed another coping mechanism. I wrote down everything that needed to be paid.
I contacted the bank and arranged for everything to be paid by direct debit from the bank account I had kept open which was in my own name.
This was time consuming, writing to various companies explaining that all bills were to be addressed to me. There were a few hiccups during this change over period but by the second month everything was settled and my account was operating successfully.
I found I could have a social life, buy what I needed and still have a small amount of money left over that I would try and save.
I would feel really guilty when I went to purchase new clothes, convincing myself that I shouldn't be spending my money in case he was watching me and thought I was being irresponsible.
It took about twelve months until I was fully

confident in managing all aspects of my finances.

I walked down the street, at every footstep I heard behind me, I would stop and look around clutching my mobile in my hand. I was convinced he was following me. A plastic carrier bag flew in front of me. I jumped, as I was startled.
When getting into my car, I would check the car park and the area immediately surrounding my car in case he was hiding behind a parked vehicle. I was expecting him to jump out, grab me and kidnap me.
At that stage in my recovery I still half expected him to follow me. I always checked the immediate surroundings I was in. I was very ritualistic in my behaviour and remained that way for a long time.

I took the bus home from work. Sitting in front of me was a young couple, both in their late teens. He appeared to be teasing her. He was calling her very unpleasant personal names, "stupid fucking bitch", "dirty whore", "fat cow", were amongst the phrases he used to insult her. He was smiling at her whist using these names.
In a flash I was back in the situation of my relationship.
The boy then began to "play fight" with his partner, pushing her back on to her seat when she sat forward, and punching her on her arm.
She was becoming distressed, telling him to stop as he was hurting her.
I couldn't bear it. I began to relive the beating I had received, flashes of the attack appeared like a

Sour Face

video playing before my eyes.

I had to get off that bus, even though I was nowhere near my bus stop.

I stopped to ask the girl if she was all right as I got up to leave the bus.

She didn't answer me. She just looked down at her feet.

Her partner glared at me. His eyes told me my interference was not welcome.

Feeling nervous I repeated my question, again no eye contact or response from the girl. He turned to me and told me to "fuck off, nosy old cow".

I felt physically sick as I watched the two of them sitting together staring at me from the window of the bus, as I headed towards home. There was nothing I could do to help that girl, I thought as I walked up the street towards my house, but I knew in my heart of hearts that I had tried. I hadn't ignored the situation, or turned a blind eye as I may have done in the past, because that would have been the easy option. Even though I hadn't wanted to get involved I had done. How can we as a society ignore bullying of any description or form? We have a duty to challenge situations we know are unacceptable.

During the first week on my own I discovered the "dark place."

I would tumble into this world whenever I was alone. Once I was in there it would take days to come back out.

A blanket of dark thoughts would surround me. Feelings of utter despair, panic, grief and loneliness were with me constantly.

I couldn't sleep; when I did go to sleep I would wake up after a few hours and then stay awake.

I didn't eat. I just wasn't hungry.

What was the point of being alive; all I did was cause the people who cared about me grief and worry.

I didn't want to get up. I wanted to stay in my sleeping bag. I only made myself get up because I didn't want to lose my job.

I didn't want to speak to anyone, what was the point?

In the "dark place", I could hide away from the world. No one judged me there. There was no pain, no fear; the silence surrounds you giving you a strange comfort.

The only drawback is that the people you care about can't come into the dark place with you. You are there on your own. You shut them out, you don't want to, but they don't understand how you need to be in the "dark place". You don't want to shut them out, you love them, but you can't have them in the "dark place", as that's your private world.

I knew I was depressed, I remembered all the signs and symptoms of depression from my training. I didn't want to go to my GP, as I was determined that I didn't want to take anti depressants pills. I confided in a friend who is a professional in the health care industry. We met every week to discuss my thoughts, feelings and fears.

My friend asked me if I had experienced similar feelings before.

After I had been in the relationship with him for

Sour Face

about six months I found myself feeling very low in mood. It dawned on me one day that I felt so unhappy. I was constantly upset. I felt that my nerves were on edge and I became very snappy towards my work mates. I couldn't remember a time when I last felt happy or relaxed. I thought these feelings were hormone related and commenced herbal treatments. I found that these tablets did improve my mood after a few months. I stopped feeling so negative about issues and could find solutions to problems I was experiencing.

My friend explained that these tablets were also effective in the treatment of mild depression. I had stopped taking them when I had begun to feel better. He had refused to let me buy them telling me that they were "too fucking expensive. There's nothing fucking wrong with you, apart from you being a mad fucking bitch".

My friend felt that I could have been suffering depression type symptoms as a result of the extremely stressful relationship I had been in.

We put coping mechanisms for me in place, mainly consisting of sticking to my routines, talking to a close friend daily, and ringing my health professional friend when I felt particularly low at any time of day or night.

My friend also discussed writing as therapy with me. I had heard about it, but I felt it wasn't relevant for me. I thought writing therapy was only for arty people who had a talent for writing. The whole idea sounded very new age. My friend explained that by writing down thoughts, memories, and how I felt about my current situation, it would help to release emotion I had suppressed over the years. We would then be able to discuss my notes each time we met.

I decided to give it a try, well I had nothing to lose, and I just wanted to feel "normal". I bought myself a red notebook and a green ink ballpoint pen, exclusively for the purpose of my writing. I wanted to use a different coloured pen from the blue or black ink I wrote in everyday.

Once I picked up the green pen the words began to flow onto the paper. I found that events, experiences, thoughts and feelings that occurred during the relationship filled the pages of my note pad. I carried the notebook with me at all times. Every time a thought came into my head, I wrote it down. I found the most thoughts came to me first thing in the morning when I could literally fill several pages with words.

As I read the words I had written, I began to come to terms with what had happened to me. I didn't intend to write about my relationship, it just happened. Memories I had either forgotten or suppressed came flooding back into my mind.

After discussing my writing with my friend I began to research the psychology behind my feelings. I became very interested in the theories behind domestic abuse. I spent months reading, writing and talking to other victims of domestic abuse.

From my scribbled, green notes a manuscript developed. I never ever dreamed that that would happen. I didn't wake up one morning and decide that I was going to write a book. It just appeared to be the natural progression for my notes to take. My friend encouraged me to continue to write and

develop my work into a manuscript. I wrote every day for ten months. I found myself getting stronger every day, because with each event I wrote down, read about and then discussed with my friend, I felt I was learning to deal with these feelings. Leaving them in the past where they belonged. This enabled me to begin the very slow journey of moving on.
I still visit the dark place, eighteen months after the relationship ended, but not on a regular basis. I no longer fully immerse myself in there. I can come out of the dark place by myself. When I feel myself slipping in there, I reach for my notebook. I find by writing down recent events, thoughts and feelings I can understand why I ended in the dark place.
I keep myself mentally and physically active. I eat as healthily as I can and still have my counselling sessions with my friend, as I need them.

As a result of being pushed up and dragged down the stairs, usually by my neck or hair, I developed a fear of the stairs, rather a fear of falling whilst on the stairs. A good friend of mine, after seeing me walk down the stairs asked me if I had ever fallen down the stairs, due to my behaviour on the staircase. I didn't have any problems with the stairs prior to meeting him.
 Going up and coming down stairs was a nightmare, particularly when people surrounded me. I panicked at the sight of them. It was like having to climb a mountain, my heart pounded and I felt sick.
I would grip the banister tight and come down

them very slowly. I make sure my feet were firmly on each stair before taking the next step. Again I wrote about these fears in my notebooks. I developed a coping mechanism for dealing with the stairs. I still have a fear of falling on the stairs, but thanks to my coping plan, the fear is manageable.

I take my time on the staircase. I always ensure that I'm not wearing heels when I go out and hold on to the banister at all times. I stay to the right hand side of the staircase and let people pass me on the left hand side.

I slowly walked down a flight of stairs in a busy city shop. Clutching on to the hand- rail, I looked around me to make sure that no one could bump into me or try and make me go faster down the stairs. This is when I really panic as I am convinced I will fall.

A man came past me. He didn't need the hand-rail. He skipped down the stairs, using the middle of the staircase. He was out of the shop before I'd reached halfway.

I left the shop feeling so envious of him. I just so hope that will be me one day, striding out in the middle of the stairs, confident in my own ability not to have a fall.

I don't know if this fear of falling on the stairs will ever leave me, but with my coping plan in place, I can now live a normal life.

Jill rang me. "Get your glad rags on. We are going out for a night on the town".

"Thanks mate. That's nice of you to think about me, but honestly, I really don't feel like going out tonight. I'm very tired. I plan on doing some of my housework jobs and having an early night. You go out with Darren. Have a good time", I replied.

"That's the same excuse you have given me every Saturday night for the past three months. To be honest with you I'm sick of your excuses. You and I are going out tonight, and that's final. I've booked the taxi to pick you up at nine o'clock. Make sure you're ready. I'll meet you at the pub". Jill hung up. I stood in the hall looking at the phone.

"Ring her back", my heart told me, "tell her you really don't feel well. You know she means well and wants to help, but you are really better off here on your own".

"Hang on a minute", my head was talking to me now, "what is the real reason why you won't go out socializing? You loved going to the pub and meeting your friends. Once you were on the dance floor, you'd be there all night. You really used to enjoy yourself. Why don't you want to do those things anymore?"

Then memories of conversations he had had with me filtered through my mind.

"You are going to a fucking club! You will look so fucking desperate. All the men in there will think you are after one thing. That's a quick fuck. You are so fucking needy. You have got to go to a club in order to find a man, because you can't survive without one. You just can't be by yourself. You are so fucking pathetic. You are so ugly. Men will laugh at you and your mate when you go into any club together. Whoever pulls you will have definitely won the pull the moose competition. How fucking stupid are you? When will you finally realise that there is only one person who will ever find you attractive, and that's me. You are an acquired taste. I don't go for classic model looks, which is why I ended up with you. "

I looked at my reflection in the hall mirror.

"Stop listening to him. He's not here. It doesn't matter what he says anymore. None of what he ever said to you was true". I said the words out loud. I didn't believe what I had just said. I'd failed abysmally to convince myself that he had lied to me.

"What the hell", I told myself in the mirror, "Jill won't take no for an answer and the cab will be here in an hour. Just get ready and go. You can always come back when you've had enough. At least Jill will have seen that you have made the effort and tried to go out".

I was very nervous as I walked into the pub, which had once been our local.

Everyone in there knew us as a couple. They were all aware that we had split up and the reasons why. We lived in a small town, news travelled very fast.

It was the first time in two and a half years that I had gone out on my own as a single woman. It felt so strange and rather uncomfortable being in surroundings we had always been in together. I kept on looking at the pub door. I expected him to come walking through it at any minute. He didn't.

None of his friends had heard from him since we had split up. Most of his friends didn't want to talk to him again, because of his violence towards me. They felt that they could no longer be friends with someone who abused women; all of his friends

Sour Face

offered me their support, which was very nice of them and also very surprising. He had always told me that his friends didn't like me, because I was very controlling and had changed him too much. They certainly never gave me that impression.

My friends came to sit with me and to offer me their support. "It's good to see you out and about".

"You are better off without him". "If you need help with anything then all you have to do is ask".

"It's so good to see you back to normal" were some of the comments I received.

I didn't think that I would ever be "normal" again. I thanked them for their words of support. They all meant well and were trying to help me in the ways they knew how.

They didn't want to know how I was really feeling or the details of what my life with him had been like. I wouldn't have told them if they had asked me. I was still so very ashamed of how I had let him treat me. Yes that was how I was thinking. I had allowed him to abuse me. It would take many more months before I accepted that the abuse wasn't my fault.

After that, I began to go out most weekends.

Every time I got ready to go out I would hear his voice in my head, telling me how ridiculous I was being.

I would still dress in the type of clothing he had chosen for me when we were together. When I went shopping for new clothes, I would take a long time choosing what to buy. I had forgotten what I liked to wear. I knew what he wanted me to look like. I would pick an item of clothing off the rail and tell myself "He'd like you in that. He always had better taste than you. He was very good with styles and colours; you always looked good in what he chose for you. What's the point in fixing something that's not broken?" So I would buy the item. Of course I know now that I was still conditioned to his way of thinking. I had two years of living and dressing as his ideal perfect woman. I had to learn to be myself again.

Word had spread round the various weekend venues I visited on a regular basis, that I was officially single. I found that men began to chat to me. Most of them I had known by sight for quite a while, but had never chatted to them as I was in a relationship.

His comments about me looking desperate and needy sprang into my head, every time someone spoke to me. I tried so hard to push these thoughts to the back of my mind. I pretended to be confident around new people. I smiled back, chatted appropriately and laughed in the right places. Yet in my heart I felt so disloyal to him, I felt like I was committing adultery.

I went on my first date six months after we had split up. Well it wasn't really a date, that's what I told myself. I went for a drink with a man I had known for a while. He liked me, found me attractive and wanted to see me again. He told me I was the type of person he had been looking for and would like us to see each other on a regular basis. It would have been so easy to start a relationship with this man. I wouldn't be lonely any more. He was pleasant and attractive enough.

I knew in my knower, that I didn't need a relationship to make me happy. Most importantly I didn't want a relationship at that time in my life. That was an enormous step on my road to recovery. I didn't want or need a man until I was ready. I would know when I was and until then I would enjoy my life and wait for the right person. This isn't the stuff of fairy tales. The right person for me was out there and until I found them I was happy and I honestly was, by myself. Of course I was lonely at times, when I'd come home from work to an empty house, but being lonely is better than being with someone you don't really care about.

This didn't mean that I was a saint or a hermit. Far from it, but for the first time in my life I was comfortable and happy living the life of a single woman.

Three years to the day of meeting him and I lay as still as I could, inside a MRI scanning machine.

The whirring noise of the machine filled the consulting rooms. My ears protected by earphones helped to dim the noise (similar to a road drill). I lay in agony as I passed through the machine, each of the twenty minutes it took to complete the process feeling like hours.

I began to experience a twisting type of throbbing pain towards the left of my cervical spine, into my shoulder approximately twelve months into the relationship. Some days the pain was so severe it would reduce me to tears. I thought the pain could be from my bad posture whilst working on the computer, or from carrying heavy shopping bags.

I tried to reduce the weight I carried on a daily

basis, and sat as upright as possible. These tactics didn't really help the pain. I just then decided that it must be due to stress or tiredness. I took painkillers when the pain was extreme and tried to ignore it as much as possible.

I began experiencing problems with my shower, which has a press button to operate it. It would take at least eight attempts at pressing the button, until the shower would turn on. I was about to call in an electrician to find out what was wrong with it, when one morning, I pressed the switch with my left hand. The shower came on immediately. I was surprised. The next day I tried to turn the shower on with my right hand. Again it wouldn't come on. I then tried using my left hand. Again, the shower came on immediately.

I then began to experience pins and needles radiating from my elbow into my forearm, across the palm of my hand and into my middle and ring fingers. This affected the grip in my hand. I would have pins and needles in my hand and arm constantly throughout the day.

The pain was also increasing. I would wake up and be in pain as soon I woke up and would get no respite from the pain all day. The pain would also wake me up at night, and I would find it very difficult to get back to sleep again.

Bernie nagged me until I went to my GP. I really thought I was wasting his time and that he would send me away with a flea in my ear. There were people who were really sick who needed his time more than I did.

He examined me thoroughly. There was a marked weakness in my right hand and arm. The pins and needles in my hand indicated that there was something wrong at with the nerve at the sixth and seventh cervical vertebrae. He decided to send me for an X ray of my neck and cervical spine.

Ten days later I was back in my doctor's surgery. The X ray results showed that there was an overgrowth of bone on the sixth and seventh vertebrae. This growth could be responsible for the pins and needles as it could be pressing down on the nerve.

The GP asked me if I had been in an accident as the extra growth on the vertebrae indicated that it could have occurred from previous fractures.

I explained that I had been physically attacked on a regular basis, which included being grabbed and dragged around the house by my neck. I also told him that I would be slammed against the wall and held there by my neck for long periods. The GP asked me if my abuser had gone to prison for the injuries he had caused. He was very surprised when I informed him he hadn't.

Due to the discomfort I was in and the weakness in my hand he decided that I needed to have an urgent MRI scan. It was important to find out what was happening to the nerve. If there was any damage, treatment needed to begin as soon as possible, to prevent muscle wasting of my right arm.

The results of the MRI scan showed that there was nerve impingement. This meant that the vertebrae had been fractured and had healed it's self as the body does so well. Unfortunately, the bone does not stop calcifying and grows downwards. This results in fingers of bone pressing down on the nerve causing the pins and needles.

He told me there were two options. I could take painkillers and be referred to a physiotherapist. If painkillers weren't effective I could look at trying antidepressants as they have been proven to be effective in the treatment of back and spine pain.

The other option open to me would be surgery. This would be the last resort, as operations on necks are not considered to be routine and can be dangerous and ineffective. I didn't want to have an operation. I also didn't want to take any type of pill that would make me sleepy, as I had to work.

He decided to refer me to the physiotherapy department of my local hospital.

Unfortunately, due to the over growth of bone on the vertebrae, I was unable to receive any physiotherapy treatment. There was a risk that any manipulation of my spine could result in the bone over growths breaking off, causing more damage to my nerve.

I was advised to purchase a nerve -stimulating machine to manage the pain, to continue to exercise gently, and to listen to my body.

If I experienced any pain whilst doing an activity, I was told to stop and rest. I was also advised to look at my seating arrangements at work, and to sit propped with pillows when I was relaxing at home.

I followed these instructions, and found that these accompanied with herbal treatments and vitamin supplements helped to manage the pain and discomfort I feel.

There is a very good chance that these bone

growths will turn into arthritis as I grow older, which may have an impact on my mobility in later life.

It angers me that he hurt me physically, causing me injuries that at the time I didn't realise I had.

That is the irony of my situation. Everything is hidden. We as victims hide the evidence of what is happening to us from other people and also most importantly from ourselves. We convince our selves that our abuse isn't happening. If you can't see a mark, well he hasn't really done any damage, there's no bruising or swelling. You are just a bit shocked, but you'll be fine. He didn't mean it.

My response to this statement would be, yes he did mean it. He had every intention of hurting you, as my abuser had every intention of hurting me. If you can't see any marks or bruises, and you are continually being abused physically over a period of time, the damage being done could be a lot worse than you could ever imagine.

During the last conversation I had with him, I told him about the injuries he had caused to my neck. I'd been advised by my solicitor to sue him for criminal damages if he made any claim on my house.

"You just do to me what you feel you have to", he mocked. "I really don't care about what happened to you. It's in the past. I've dealt with it. I can't believe you would drag the past up after all this time. I know you are doing this just to hurt me. You've found out that I've got another partner and we are really happy. You are just jealous".

"All I care about is the money you owe me", he declared. "The money is all that I am interested in".

Those words summed up exactly what he thought about me and our so- called relationship.

He showed no remorse for how he had hurt me physically. He had put me in the box marked "the past" and firmly closed the lid.

I had repeatedly told myself that he didn't care how he'd treated me. The extensive research I'd carried out had confirmed those thoughts.

But as a human being, who had cared about this person, I needed to believe that he was sorry for his behaviour. If he wasn't then he really was inhuman. His reaction to my injuries confirmed that he was indeed that. In fact I would go one step further and say that his reaction to the injuries he had caused illustrates that he is in fact a beast.

Sour Face

A Saturday morning in December

A trail of my breath followed behind me as I walked towards the train station. I snuggled into the hood of my coat as the cold air stung my face. I began to walk faster as I was already late.

I ran across the road, squinting as the winter sun shone directly into my eyes.

I ran up the steps and pushed open the heavy glass door leading into the train station. My heart pounded with excitement.

Standing there was the person I had been looking for, for a long time.

He is warm, funny, and intelligent. He has a real caring nature, is rather a chatterbox, and is cute looking. I had found someone who fully understood what they were letting themselves in for, by starting a relationship with a recovering victim of domestic abuse.

I had to try and have a relationship again. If I didn't then he would have won.

I had reflected on my previous relationships in great detail. I was determined not to make the same mistakes again. This time my approach to finding a suitable partner would be different.

I had been very fussy. I had drawn up a mental list of attributes the person I wanted to be with had to have. There was no compromise. I was brutal in my dismissal of unsuitable men.

I was determined that I would not settle for second best.

Then I met Charlie.

He is no knight in shining armour. He's not going to take me away on his white horse into the sunset and make everything that was wrong in my life right. This is real life, where you have to work hard for everything you want and that includes relationships.

We both know life won't be easy for us. I am still on the road to recovery. There are still issues that only I can address and work through. I recognise my problem areas and with the help of my writing, and my ability to communicate my feelings honestly and effectively, I am convinced I will be able eventually to put my past behind me.

In Charlie I have met a person who will do his best to support me, no matter how hard life gets. We are both willing to take a chance on each other.

We will both make mistakes. We will do each other's heads in. But in Charlie I have met a person who, I really trust and I never thought I would trust a man again. I didn't want to trust a man again, if I'm honest. It was easier to think that all men are bastards. You don't get hurt again then.

For a split second I stand still looking at Charlie, who looks back with a twinkle in his eye as he smiles at me. I smile back at him as I walk towards him.

Sour Face

Two Years Later.

Writing Sour Face was the beginning of my journey from victim to survivor.

The journey has been long, tough at times and I'm under no illusion that the journey is over. I don't know if it will ever be.

I have met some fantastic people on the road I have travelled.

Among them are survivors who are helping each other, and professionals who are helping victims to become survivors. Both of these groups of people offer great services despite limited finances and restricted manpower.

One group of women in particular who are committed to empowering victims have both my admiration and support.

I have been fortunate to meet with MP's and local councillors who have been supportive of both my work and me. I have also been ignored and patronised by other councillors and some women's organisations.

The current government asked for the views of survivors of domestic abuse. They carried out an e forum asking for first hand accounts of domestic abuse by survivors. They used Sour Face as background reading. The fact that my work has been used in this way continues to amaze me.

I believe the only way that society can change its views on domestic abuse is if survivors share their experiences with the general public. This will educate society and raise the awareness of domestic abuse.

We need to smash the stereotypes and destroy

the myths that surround this subject.

I know it's not easy to tell the world what happened. I really believe with all of my heart that the more survivors who do, the more society will listen. They will have to. We as survivors are not hiding away any longer. We need to be heard.

I have developed a scheme of raising the awareness of domestic abuse within the work place. It's about to be piloted within the area I work, thanks to the terrific support of my line managers and peers.

Life for me at the moment is positive. I continue to write on a regular basis .I find great personal comfort from the practise of my faith. This is extremely important to me. I remain mentally well and strong most of the time. I still have the love and support of my wonderful children to thank for that.

Charlie and I remain together and plan to marry next year. Our relationship is strong and loving due to our mutual respect and our ability and willingness to communicate openly with each other. I still have issues but we work through them together.

Yes, we both have made mistakes and we do each other's heads in at times. This remains a real life relationship. But so far there has not been anything that we have been unable to sort out together.

So is the conclusion of this story that I lived happy ever after?

My life is certainly happier than it was two years ago. Then I was a victim of domestic abuse. Now I am a survivor.

Reference

Dutton. D.G (2007). The abusive personality (Violence and control in intimate relationships). Second edition.

Dutton, D.G & Painter S.L (1993). The battered women's syndrome: effects of severity and intermittency of abuse. American journal of orthopsychiatry, 63(4), 614-22.

Carr and Van Deusen, (2002). The relationship between family of origin violence and dating violence in college men. Journal of interpersonal violence.17 (6) 630- 646.

Hansen, D.J. Alcohol problems and solutions. Website, 1997-2007.

Hidden Hurt website 2007.

Hall, R. (1985). Ask any woman, a London inquiry into rape and sexual assault. Falling wall press. Bristol.

Jaffe, P.G., Wolfe, DA. Telford, A and Austin, G. (1986) the impact of police charges in incidents of wife abuse. Journal of family violence, 1 (1): 37-49.

Mullendender, A. (1996). Rethinking domestic violence: the social work and probation response. London; Routledge.

Nicholas, S. Povey D, Walker A, & Kershaw C. (2004- 2005). Crime in England and Wales. Home office.

Forensic Psychology Practise Ltd. (1999) Domestic Violence, a practitioner's portfolio.

Stark, S. & Flint craft A. (1997). Women at risk. Domestic violence and women's health. Journal of marriage and the family. 59(4): 1023-1036

Symmonds, D., (1980) "The second injury to victims" and "Acute responses of victims to terror". Evaluation and change. Special Issue, 36-41.

The London domestic violence strategy. 2001. Greater London authority.

Walker, L.E. (1979) the battered woman. New York; Harper and Row.

Yllo, K. (1993) through a feminist lens: gender, power and violence. In R.J Gelles and DR Loseke (EDS) current controversies on family violence. Newbury Park, CA: Sage, pp.47-62

www.ingramcontent.com/pod-product-compliance
Lightning Source LLC
Chambersburg PA
CBHW031138160426
43193CB00008B/179